STRENGTH
FOR·THE
FRAGILE
SPIRIT

ROBERT A. SCHULLER

STRENGTH
FOR·THE
FRAGILE
SPIRIT

THOMAS NELSON PUBLISHERS
Nashville

Published in Nashville, Tennessee, by Thomas Nelson, Inc. and distributed in Canada by Lawson Falle, Ltd., Cambridge, Ontario.

Printed in the United States of America.

Scripture quotations are from THE NEW KING JAMES VERSION of the Bible. Copyright © 1979, 1980, 1982, Thomas Nelson, Inc., Publishers.

ISBN 0-8407-7225-4

Before you can effectively read a written passage to someone, you must comprehend its message. Your understanding and your feelings about the written words will be expressed both verbally and non-verbally through your intonations and body language.

This is the teaching of John Holland, my professor of oral reading at Fuller Theological Seminary. Through his insistence, I read and re-read Isaiah 40, both silently and aloud, until I comprehended its message. When I finally grasped its meaning, I was able to communicate orally that passage to my classmates.

So it is my honor to dedicate this book to John Holland for introducing me to this great chapter.

Contents

1   Strength for the Fragile Spirit 11
2   Speak Tenderly 25
3   Forgiving and Forgetting 47
4   Searching for Peace 69
5   Can You Hear the News? 95
6   Whom Do You Trust? 117
7   Small Among Giants 139
8   Reason with Yourself 163
9   Waiting on the Lord 183
    Notes 207

STRENGTH
FOR·THE
FRAGILE
SPIRIT

Chapter 1

Strength for the Fragile Spirit

Cindy, a young woman of twenty-six, has arthritis. She was told that the medication she must take would make it impossible for her and her husband to have children. So they adopted a lively two-year-old, and then unexpectedly she became pregnant. Then, suddenly, her condition deteriorated. Because her hands became almost useless, she lost her job. She has already undergone several operations on her hands, and the situation is still no better. She cannot even give her children baths without help. Beyond worrying about bills and the daily tasks she now finds impossible, she also must face the limitations and pain the arthritis increasingly forces upon her.

Dan is an average guy. In a life as normal as the next person's, he gave his time to the church, to his work, and to his family. Then he noticed that his teenager was becoming more and more distant. His son had always been such a good kid that he never thought twice about it. His friends seemed so clean-cut, the cream of the crop. One day, his son's school called. His son had been caught selling and using drugs with several of his friends. They were caught when his son passed out in the bathroom. An ambulance had been called. His son was at the hospital, and so were the policemen.

Joy is another who has felt the wear and tear, the confusion, of living today. Joy had always had someone to rely on. She married Joe right out of high school, and all she wanted was a family, a nice house, and an average, safe life. And that's what she got for ten years. Her life was a busy round of PTA, church, and motherly duties. She and Joe were both too busy, but she thought their life together was a happy one.

Something was eating at Joe, and Joy didn't exactly know what it was. But she knew she could rely on Joe. He was such a good man. Everybody said so.

Then Joe left her. He cried, but he left her. Joy moved herself and the kids back into her mother's home while trying to cope with the shock. But she found that she couldn't stand to look at her children. She blamed them for Joe's leaving. She couldn't stand to think about praying because she blamed God for allowing it to happen. If she couldn't rely on Joe and she couldn't rely on God to keep her from such harm, then whom could she rely on?

And that's when she met Mike. He was muscular and tall and seemed interested in her. She began to flirt with him, and he responded. And she felt wonderful. He would make her feel happy again. When Mike offered to take her in, she accepted. She left her children with her mother—just for a while, she told herself. She was entitled to a little happiness.

What followed was a nightmare. Mike tired of her quickly, but she was obsessed. The more he verbally abused her, the more she was determined to please him. She had to make this work. And then Mike told her to leave. She refused, so Mike left.

Joy tried to find him, but he vanished. Then, slowly, she began to come to her senses. She had been away from her mother and children for months. As she

*Exercise your spirit
and watch it
mature.*

thought of them, she felt as if she were waking from a dream. She called her mother. Her mother sounded edgy and nervous—and very angry. She told Joy she could not handle her kids any longer. They were both having troubles at school, her son's so severe that he had just taken a swing at his teacher and been expelled. What had she done to her kids? she wondered. She had more than once in the last few days thought of taking her own life, something her religious upbringing had never allowed her to contemplate before. Could she handle what lay ahead? She felt so fragile. How could she have been so wrong? And now, how could she ever go back and face her mother and her children?

These friends of mine are no different from you and me, struggling to keep their fragile spirits strong through the wear and tear of what we call living in this troubled modern world.

I'd like to say that we are immune to such threats to our spirits. I'd like to say that our spirits aren't fragile.

But it's not so. All we have is a chance to make our wear and tear a source of strength, a layering of spiritual toughness that belies the tender spirit that dwells and flourishes underneath. That is our potential—what our faith can give us, through right choices and wrong ones.

Isaiah knew that. And this tough but tender old bird offers us some insight into just how to pull off this balancing act in one of the most famous chapters in the Bible, Isaiah 40. It is a piece of literature, a wonderful exposition of the sovereignty of God, and it offers us a beautiful understanding of God's comforting and strengthening of his ordinary folks like us, his people.

Isaiah was quite a man. He's been called the prince of the Old Testament, the greatest of the Hebrew prophets, the evangelist of the Old Testament, his words and prophecies ranking at the very top in importance. Every Jewish child in Christ's day knew Isaiah's words by heart, no doubt. He's quoted more times in the New Testament than any other Old Testament writer. Twenty-one quotations specifically refer to him. Fifty times the New Testament writers use quotations from Isaiah, and his words are alluded to over 250 times. Christ actually started his public ministry with a quotation from Isaiah[1] and quoted him off-handedly in the parable of the sower, knowing quite well that his listeners knew where the quotation came from.[2]

I know of no better counselor in the Bible, or even today, to guide us through tough times. That's why I recommend that people in my church read and reread (and sometimes even memorize) Isaiah 40 when they are facing difficult problems.

"Isaiah knew the same feelings of failure and pain you suffer now," I tell them. "Don't think of him as a bedraggled man of the wilderness. He was far from it."

Isaiah was probably a cousin of the king at the time, his father a brother of the king. So he no doubt had the run of the palace as a child and was looking forward to a life of ease and power when God called him to help a nation gone astray, in need of guidance, forgiveness, comfort, and encouragement in their tough, trouble-ridden world. Isaiah knew the sacrifice of commitment; he's not encouraging us from the ease of a gilded couch.

Encouragement, guidance, forgiveness, comfort—who doesn't need a gallon of each of these.

Joy's fragile spirit needed them. After several days on the brink of taking her own life, something incredible happened to Joy. At the grocery store, she bumped into an old friend, Penny, whom she had not seen in years. Joy had begun to look so rough that her friend didn't recognize her. When Penny asked how she and her family were doing, Joy burst into tears, unable to respond. Penny looked around the store, then back at her friend who was out of control for reasons Penny did not know. So Penny gently took Joy's arm and led her to Penny's car. There, in private, Penny quietly took Joy in her arms and comforted her.

In a moment, Joy told the whole story for the first time, including her feelings of guilt over leaving her children, over moving in with Mike, over Joe's leaving, even over turning a deaf ear to God.

And how did Penny respond? She asked Joy if she thought God could forgive her. Joy hesitated, then answered, "Yes. I know he can. It's whether I can forgive myself."

Penny smiled and squeezed her friend's arm. "You will. Give yourself a break. Who are you not to forgive yourself when God has forgiven you?"

That made Joy smile.

"Why do you think all this happened?" Penny asked.

Joy frowned a moment, then sighed. "I've been thinking about that one for quite a while now. I don't know. I think it had something to do with suddenly not trusting God. If Joe could desert me, then why couldn't God? I just couldn't believe God was in control through such pain, and I didn't wait long enough to find out."

Then Penny asked her friend what she wanted to do and what she thought she should do. Joy knew the answer to both questions. So did Penny. And Penny drove Joy back to her mother's.

Living, now or in Isaiah's time, has its share of problems. Perhaps we're asking the same sorts of questions as those who first heard Isaiah's words, too:

How do we live in this hard world?

Whom can we rely on?

What difference does being a Christian make when we hurt?

Where do we find comfort and peace?

How can we keep from making wrong, hurtful choices?

The answers to those all-important questions lie in things we should know about our God, about our faith, and about ourselves if we are to become the persons we are meant to be in this tough and trouble-ridden world.

My wife, Donna, and I are very interested in physical fitness. We have participated in aerobic classes, weight training, and jogging. We know from personal experience that if we want to have strong bodies we must exercise. There are no shortcuts. We don't have any alternatives. The cliché "If you don't use it, you lose it" runs very true when it comes to building muscle and endurance. No one can be physically fit without exercising. I would encourage everyone to ask his doctor for some physical exercises. It's fun and you will feel better.

Spiritual fitness is much the same way. In order to strengthen our spirits we need to exercise them. There are no shortcuts. No one can gain spiritual fitness without spiritual exercises. Isaiah reminds us of eight important exercises that anyone can use to develop strength and endurance for their spirit (see page 21).

Eight Exercises to Strengthen Our Fragile Spirits

1. *Speak comfort*—to yourself and to others.
2. *Forgive and give* double pardon to those who harm you.
3. *Generate* the peace that makes your crooked places straight.
4. *Believe* in the fact that God is in control.
5. *Trust* the One who measures the waters in the palm of his hand.
6. *Feel free and comfortable* in a room full of giants.
7. *Test* the God who neither faints nor is weary.
8. *Wait on the Lord* so that you can run and not be weary, walk and not faint.

In the chapters ahead, we will discuss each of these exercises and Isaiah's instructions for finding them. The exercises that unlock the strength for a fragile spirit have always been there, just as God has always been there, yet many of us never use them. Each exercise has a power to revitalize a wounded, suffering spirit. Each one brings us closer to God himself.

Joy experienced the power of Isaiah's exercises. Through Penny's comfort, she was able to confront her problem; through accepting forgiveness, she was able to look ahead; through trusting once again, she could see that God's control starts with learning to wait on the Lord. And with that, she was able to return to her children, face the problems ahead, and start over.

It's true. Isaiah's exercises work. They have worked in my own spirit. Through my own tough times and through the battering of the fragile spirits of many fine Christian friends, I have seen them work. Isaiah has hit the bull's-eye on how to deal with life in a cruel and capricious world. The evidence is in the lives of Christians who are learning to triumph even through suffering.

You'll read about such people in these pages, how they have discovered the strength for their fragile spirits, and you'll begin to understand what it takes to plug that power into your own lives. The three people described in the opening of this book have learned to find that strength. And so can you.

No matter what pain, what trouble, what suffering is robbing you of your spiritual strength, don't despair. There is ample strength for our fragile spirits. The warfare of your soul can be won. My prayer for you is that the pages ahead will transform your days into ones of triumph and perseverance as you tap into God's power and peace.

"Comfort, yes, comfort My people!"
Says your God.

—*Isaiah 40:1*

Chapter 2

Speak
Tenderly

Gene had always been a take-charge type of guy. He had little sympathy for softness. He decided what had to be done and he did it. In a positive person like Gene, that attitude had always been an asset in his work and even in his family. Everyone knew Gene could handle anything. No one coddled him. He was a rock.

Then Gene had his first heart attack. He was hospitalized for a couple of days. His family was worried about him, but Gene shrugged it off. He would slow down a bit, watch his diet, and basically forget that it happened. He was still a rock.

Then he had his second heart attack. And then his third. He was diagnosed with a condition that caused mild heart attacks. He was told that no matter what he did, he would continue to have them, off and on, for the rest of his life. He could not deny his weakness anymore: physically he was no longer a rock. At any moment now, he could be made helpless with a heart scare, dependent on whoever was near. Now his whole life was tilted. He was in a hospital room—being "coddled," he grunted. He hated it. But as he contemplated a weaker and weaker future, this tough man needed comforting for the first time in his life.

Comfort Ye

Picture Isaiah. Can you? He is probably an old man. Flowing beard. Once regal robe, torn and dirty. He may be sitting on hay in a prison cell, coughing from the damp, nursing his bruised and beaten body. Perhaps he is sitting at a makeshift table, using a crude pencil to scratch out his thoughts in letter form. Or maybe he is hiding in one of the many caves in the wilderness, sending words to his countrymen scattered everywhere.

And his first words to his friends are, "Comfort ye." The message is one we need to hear now just as desperately as did the people then. From its opening words, it speaks to us.

Comfort.

The people to whom he was writing were fellow Israelites, a people divided and in trouble. They were living in a crucial time for God's people, and they were in many ways without comfort at all.[1]

Tough Times

Two dramatic events in Isaiah's era inspired his writing. Both of them deal with failure.

Isaiah was born in a prosperous time for Israel. Yes, they had already split into the two kingdoms, the Northern Kingdom known as Israel, with its capital of Samaria, and the Southern Kingdom called Judah, with its capital of Jerusalem. Things hadn't been so good for the Israelites since the golden era of David and Solomon.

But even so, the people had grown a bit fat and sassy, too confident in their own powers. The prophet Amos, who ministered to the Northern Kingdom, called the women "cows" because of their self-indulgence, and he was merciless when it came to their debauchery.[2] Isaiah, who spent his ministry preaching to the Southern Kingdom, Judah, could be just as forthright.

Comfort is a
by-product of
knowing whose
we are.

Then, after years of failed attempts, the Assyrians captured the Northern Kingdom and made repeated sweeps over the land, decimating the population by carrying off the rich and strong into slavery while depositing prisoners from other lands on Northern Kingdom soil.

Those who were left behind intermarried with the foreigners, and the Samaritan nation began. The Jewish prejudice against the interracial Samaritans, so well-known in the New Testament, began here.

During all this, Judah, the Southern Kingdom, which Isaiah spent his life preaching to, resisted the Assyrian advances. They themselves grew just as smug, lax, and self-satisfied, though. Oh, they were on top of the world economically and militarily. But the prosperity was anything but good for the moral and social climate. In the years ahead, they would begin a slide that would finally destroy them. Isaiah knew it and preached against it. The word *degenerate* is used by many scholars to describe the true nature of the remaining nation of Israel. The rich were getting richer on the backs of the poor. The judges were corrupt, and almost everyone indulged in "drunkenness" and "revelry."

It's not that they weren't "religious." When it came to "going to church," keeping the rituals, ceremonies, and rules of the faith, they were outstanding. In other words, Saturday night had nothing to do with Sunday morning.

Then, as invaders began to make headway into their land, the kings, against the advice of Isaiah, began to make alliances with other nations to fend off the Philistines and Persians and others always pushing at their borders, appeasing them even to the point of bringing their pagan gods into the country.

Of course, Isaiah was not making friends during all this. Not being the least bit shy, he was rebuking kings as well as paupers. God had told him what was going to happen to his people if they didn't come "clean." And Isaiah told them, "Come now and let us reason together . . . though your sins are like scarlet, they shall be as white as snow."[3] But things did not change.

Then one day in 586 B.C., the Babylonians, who had conquered the Assyrians, finally succeeded in defeating Judah's armies. Jerusalem was destroyed, ripped apart. The Babylonians were so angry by the time they finally conquered the city that they laid the place bare, flattening houses, slaughtering livestock, burning crops, killing or capturing as they saw fit. Again the strong were taken off in chains. The weak cowered behind the rubble of brick and clay, left to eke out a living under foreign rule.

These were not happy times to be an Israelite. The Israelites were under tremendous pressure. The best and the brightest were in exile, leaving a land divided and conquered. Those who were left worried that no matter how hard they worked to rebuild and replant, their enemies could fling themselves down into the Promised Land and drag anyone they wanted into slavery, back to the countries we know today as Iraq and Iran.

As Isaiah wrote, this was the reality of the Israelites' every waking moment. The ones who were left behind had very little to keep them going. Even their temple was gone. Chances are the prophet Isaiah himself was bound and taken into captivity. He may have been in bondage when he wrote these words back to the people in Jerusalem. Tradition tells us that he met his death in a gruesome way—being sawed in two by a king who grew tired of listening to him.

What, though, were the first words from his own pen? " 'Comfort my people,' says your God." "Speak tenderly" is the way the American Standard Version of the Bible translates it.

These few words had to be music to the exiles' ears. Isaiah was telling them not only that God was coming to pull his people back together, make the crooked straight, and smooth the rough places, but that Israel should speak tenderly to itself. The members of the Northern Kingdom known as Israel should reach out to the members of the Southern Kingdom, Judah, and vice versa, wherever their brothers might be. Both were decimated; both thought themselves beyond repair and reconciliation. The prophet, whose words were not always welcome during the fat and sassy days, was telling them that there is hope. God is coming. Take comfort and give it.

Tough Times Today

It's all too easy to draw comparisons with God's people then and God's people now. Though we might look prosperous and though we have more than enough to get us by materially, many of us are suffering intense private pain. Gene had everything a man could want before his heart attacks, and he felt invincible until his body told him otherwise. His pain was harder on his psyche than on his body, though. He, like the Israelites, was more wounded inside than out.

But if the comparison can be made for our suffering, it can also be made for our hope. Think about Isaiah writing just to you. You can be comforted in your problems, Isaiah is saying. Be comforted. Remember whose you are. Take it easy on yourselves and on those around you. God loves you very much.

That hope in the power of comfort is waiting to be tapped into. How, exactly, then do you *do* it? Dr. Chris Knippers, the staff psychologist at Rancho Capistrano Church, knows the power of comfort and how to tap into this power.

You Are Safe

Chris was walking in a Beverly Hills park in Los Angeles with a date one night. He and his date were about to cross a busy intersection when they heard a voice behind them say, "I've got a gun, and I'm going to shoot you both."

At first, Chris thought it was a joke and turned around. There, staring at them, was a wild man—a huge man with dirty, disheveled clothes and hair, his eyes darting back and forth. He was holding a paper sack. He leaned closer to Chris and said, "I've got a gun in this bag and I'm going to take it out and I'm going to shoot both of you."

Chris thought that if he and his date would cross the street, the whole thing would blow over. But the light continued to stay red. The man had moved closer to Chris and was yelling right in his face. Realizing that this man was obviously schizophrenic and frightened, Chris knew what to do. Chris leaned close to the man and said, "You're safe. Nobody's going to hurt you. You're fine."

The man dropped the bag and started to whine,

"Everybody's been picking on me. Nobody will leave me alone. I just can't stand it anymore." In a second, he had dropped the crazed gunman act and become a little child.

Breathe Again

Chris knew a secret that all of us need to hear. Comfort is powerful. To comfort someone is to be able to transform that person. To comfort ourselves is to transform ourselves. The word *comfort* in Hebrew means "to breathe again."

Try a little experiment. Take a deep breath. Hold it a few seconds. Now, let it out. How do you feel? That new breath felt good, didn't it? It's almost as if with each breath we are beginning again, refreshed. That's the idea of comfort.

When I was in junior high, I used to play a game in the swimming pool. I saw how far I could swim without having to take a breath. I swam back and forth, back and forth, until my chest started to hurt and I got a little light-headed and my lungs began to feel as if they would explode. That was the moment I knew I had better take a breath fast. I surfaced and swam over to the side of the pool to hold on until I caught my breath. I'll never forget the comfort that piece of cement gave to me as I was breathing again, my lungs filling up anew.

To breathe again—we should be that sort of comfort to ourselves.

Why Should We Be Comforted?

Speaking tenderly to ourselves works all by itself for a while. There is power in "breathing again." But there has to be a good reason behind comfort or it will not last. What then is Isaiah's reason for our being comforted?

As a young child in Sunday school, I learned something called the Heidelberg Catechism, a fancy name for a method of Christian instruction, which consists of a series of questions and answers that teach fundamental truths of our faith. The very first question I memorized was: "What is thy only comfort in life and death?"

A powerful question. A question all of us want answered. The answer I was taught was just as powerful.

What is my only comfort? The answer is, "I belong."

We all want to belong. All through our school days we want to belong to the "in" crowd, to the best organizations. We want to feel a part of the best, the brightest, the most exciting groups. We want to feel a sense of belonging, whether it be to family or friends or careers. It's a need that we never outgrow.

But the kind of belonging that Isaiah is talking about is the best, the brightest, the most permanent kind. What does he say in that first verse? "Comfort, yes, comfort My people," says your God.

Comfort whose people? *My* people. We belong, body and soul, not to ourselves, but to God. What a comfort it is to have that niche, to know where we are in the grand scheme of life. That is belonging. In that niche, we can grow and be nourished through any warfare of the soul our fragile spirits may be fighting.

Where We Belong

In college, I studied biology. We studied the biological niche of plant life in detail. On one field trip, we went to the beaches around Lake Michigan. The sand dunes in some areas are huge. As we climbed to the top of those dunes, we saw scrub brush; then farther on, we saw that the plant life changed as the conditions of the soil changed.

If we had taken the plant life that was there, torn it away, and planted a new type of plant—corn, for instance—it would have taken an enormous amount of human resources and energy to make it grow. But if we left the area alone, in due time, exactly the same species of plants that we had ripped out and thrown away would take hold again, in the very same location, its natural niche.

It is the same with human beings. God created us for himself, and our natural human niche is with him. There cannot be comfort or understanding until we find that niche. But when we nestle into that place we were intended, under God's arm, then comfort can take its rightful place in our lives, no matter what the struggle.

In Hebrew there's a tense to talk about an action in time—one that says the action began in the past and ends in the present. The tense that Isaiah uses, though, is one that means the action—the comforting—begins somewhere in the past, it will be in the present, and it will be there the day after tomorrow and the day after the day after tomorrow. It will always *be*. The word "comfort" as used here, was, is, and will always be.

Now that is comfort. Comfort began before the prophet Isaiah uttered those words for the very first time, six hundred years before Christ was born. It was real at the moment of his writing about it; it is real now; and it will go on until the day that Christ comes back.

"Comfort, yes, comfort My people. . . . Speak comfort to Jerusalem, and cry out to her."

Doing Comfort

Yet there is a call for us to comfort as well as be comforted. God told Isaiah to comfort the Israelites. Then God told his people to comfort each other. God is also, then, calling us to comfort our friends and relatives. We don't need to wait to be comforted before we comfort. When God said, "Comfort my people, speak tenderly to her," he was telling those of the Northern Kingdom to reach out to their brothers of the Southern Kingdom, while they waited in their own foreign conditions—and vice versa. They were to prepare for God's coming back by comforting, reaching out to each other—by reconciling and healing.

Tough Comfort

In the opening story of this chapter, Gene, the tough, confident man who had prided himself on his rocklike attitude, found himself in the hospital, facing a life of dependence and what he called "coddling." His doctor, knowing that he would not rest at home, had forced him to stay in the hospital until further notice, and it was driving Gene crazy. There he was totally dependent, and the care he was being given, the comforting and nursing of the hospital staff, only irritated him. He saw them as the first intolerable steps toward his own softness. So when the perky young nurse would pop in the door and cheerily ask how he was doing, he would only growl.

"What does it look like?" he'd say, which would stop the nurse in her tracks. Then the nurse caught on and began administering a kind of tough comfort, verbally poking him, making him seem more like a headache to her. He liked that, and he began to like her.

Then, one afternoon, Gene's monitors went wild at the nurses' station. The nurse rushed in and, seeing that Gene was unable to catch his breath, called for a doctor and grabbed Gene's rough hand and held it. For the first time, Gene allowed it. He was still holding her hand ten minutes later when the scare was over. She never moved.

Then slowly she pulled her hand away, looked him in the eyes a moment, then walked out the door.

The nurse was gone for several days after that, and no one told Gene why. Gene didn't ask. At the end of the week, she was back. During her first trip in to see Gene, neither of them said anything. Then on her second round, Gene said, "You were gone."

"What?" she said. "Oh yeah. A little family trouble." And she turned to go.

"What kind of family trouble?" he said quietly.

At first, she thought he just wanted to give her a hard time again, but something in his voice made her stop and turn back toward him.

"What kind of family trouble?" he repeated, with a half smile. "I happen to have a family who thinks I'm good at solving problems. Maybe I can help."

And with that, the nurse smiled, checked her watch, and pulled up a chair.

Speak Tenderly

For all his toughness, Gene had learned the power of comfort—in taking it and in giving it. It is amazing how through our suffering or through the suffering of those around us, we can become attuned to comfort's power.

Gene's son Tom, a young man in his late twenties, had seen his father deal with his heart problems for some time. He knew the anxiety each attack produced, the helplessness both his father and mother felt, especially when it happened in public. He didn't realize that his sorrow about his father's illness was preparing him to comfort others.

One night Tom took a date to a dinner theater and halfway through the play, he saw a man get up and leave the performance with his wife following hurriedly behind. Tom recognized the symptoms immediately—the man was having heart problems just like his father's. Without another thought, Tom got up and followed them outside. They had called an ambulance, and by that time it had arrived. Tom saw that the man's wife was quite flustered, so he offered to drive her to the hospital to be with her husband. He had never met this woman before. She was a complete stranger, but Tom and his date left the theater, drove the woman to the hospital, and stayed with her the entire time the man was being tested.

When it turned out to be a false alarm, Tom and his date offered to drive the couple back to their car at the theater. They accepted, and in a few minutes, they were back at the dinner theater, saying good night.

What a wonderful, comforting gesture for that young man to perform. But the interesting fact is that Tom was also comforting himself. In his act of comfort, Tom was able to feel comforted that somebody else might do the same for his mother and father. He received comfort by giving it.

It's that old paradox of the New Testament. By giving, Jesus says, we receive. It's one of the more interesting ironies of the Christian life. By giving of his evening, Tom literally and figuratively received. Actually, it might even have been detrimental to Tom if he had not reached out to that couple. How do you think he would have felt if he had stayed at the play? Chances are good that he would have worried about the couple all through the performance, and he would not have been comfortable sitting there trying to enjoy himself.

Isaiah is reminding us that comfort is active as well as passive, a fact Tom discovered.

Comfort My People

Both Gene and his son Tom sensed a key concept in Isaiah's words. Early in his book, Isaiah talks about the fact that we need to learn to do good.[4] That sounds strange, doesn't it? I was always under the impression that being good is within itself a very simple thing to do. Don't you simply avoid evil and bad things? Obviously not. Being good and doing good are far more than not being bad or doing bad things. If we sit and do nothing at all, are we being good? No, we are just not being bad.

The same can be said for comfort. We don't become good. Instead we learn to *do* good. We don't learn to be comforted; we learn to do comfort.

As we mentioned earlier, it's an active, not a passive, word. It's not saying, "I'm comfortable." It's being comforted by learning how to comfort.

Have you ever noticed that no matter how comfortable you can get, if you stay in that position long enough, it won't be comfortable anymore? Try it. The fact is, in any position you take, you are only comfortable to a point. If you sit in the softest, plushiest, most well-designed chair long enough, no matter how you felt when you first sat down, your bottom will soon become sore, your back will get stiff, your stomach will start to growl, you'll get a headache from lack of sugar, and soon, if you are forced to stay, sitting in that soft, plush chair will become torturous.

We cannot be in a constant state of comfort. We are built for action. We have to be doing something. God never meant us to sit our lives away, striving only not to do wrong. Instead, he expects us to always be moving, acting, and when necessary comforting ourselves and others.

Learning from Pain

But how can you move when you hurt?

You may be hurting emotionally or physically; either way you may feel that you cannot move an inch, cannot comfort yourself or anyone else, because you can't think of anything but your own pain.

This may sound insane, but pain actually wakes us up to comforting in a very real way. Good actually can come from our pain.

As with most things, it depends on our attitude.

I know an older man who, right after retiring, acquired a health problem that kept him off his feet. He had been an active man and did not want to retire. That was enough to make him depressed. But then his wife died, and even though his health now allowed him to get around, he just stayed in bed. Weeks went by, and he wouldn't leave his room. The doctor told him he should get up and around or within a matter of weeks his muscles might deteriorate to the point that he would be forced to stay in bed permanently. His son tried everything to pull his father out of his inward fixation, but to no avail. So the son took a drastic step and decided to put him into a rest home, thinking that might shock his father out of his self-imposed prison.

It didn't. Soon the man was an actual invalid. He allowed his emotional pain to cripple him for real, and it has taken an awful toll on his life.

I know another man who fell six stories in a mountain-climbing accident. He got up and miraculously walked out of the wilderness to a hospital, not feeling much pain at all. Twenty-four hours later, though, he could not move a muscle. The shock had worn off, and he learned that the fall had compressed every muscle, every ligament, every vertebra in his back. He has been told that by the time he reaches retirement age he will probably be in a wheelchair. He has been told that the excruciating pain he feels every morning will never go away. But he has set his stereo to play rousing, inspiring music, like the theme from the movie *Rocky*, and every morning, pain or no, he gets up and he rides his bike. Every day, he continues to hike into the hills around his house and, in doing so, inspires others to live to the limit.

We Americans strive to avoid suffering and pain in a wrong-thinking effort to be comfortable. Being comfortable, as we mentioned, is quite different from being comforted. Much-loved author and speaker E. Stanley Jones once explained the oriental religion Buddhism as a faith based on how to avoid pain and suffering in life. The Buddhists cope with suffering by elevating themselves to a state of nothingness. Only there, they believe, can they receive the enlightenment barred by the pain and suffering of this life.

But I believe such a place would be like death. Nothingness has no feeling. There may not be pain, but there is no joy either. There is none of the wisdom that comes with learning to cope with our pain, and there is certainly no helping others, which actually makes such an attempt quite selfish. Therefore, I am willing to suffer a little here and there to know joy and wisdom.

True comfort is not a state of being, but a state of mind. When we understand that, we realize that pain is not meaningless at all.

In the December 1988 issue of *Psychology Today* there was an article about this very concept. Psychologists at the University of Virginia Medical Center showed a video to a group of chronic pain patients before they were given treatment. The video made three points about pain:

1) It is important to remain mobile because inactivity makes pain worse.

2) Patients should learn to manage pain instead of expecting a cure.

3) Radical treatment such as surgery usually will not help.

The viewers' response was quite unusual. Those who rejected the ideas in the video showed a marked increase in pain during treatment. Those who accepted the ideas as fact and decided to live their lives as successfully as possible through their pain showed a more positive attitude and resumed almost normal lives as they coped and accepted.[5]

But just as Gene learned to comfort from his own pain and his son Tom learned how to comfort through the pain of watching his father suffer, so it is with us. We can take our pain and make it teach us empathy, teach us the hard lesson of comfort.

Even though it may not be a natural response, I believe that the impulse to comfort is there within us, God-given and waiting to be tapped.

That kind of comfort is your gift from a sovereign God, Isaiah wants you to remember that. Comfort each other. Speak tenderly. Know you belong. Know that you can breathe again. That's the way it always was, is, and will be, no matter what you and your fragile spirit may suffer at this moment. Believe it. It's true. Be comforted.

"Speak comfort to Jerusalem, and cry out to her.
That her warfare is ended,
That her iniquity is pardoned;
For she has received from the LORD's hand
Double for all her sins."

—Isaiah 40:2

Chapter 3

Forgiving
and
Forgetting

A young friend of mine—I'll call her Susan—has endured more by age twenty-five than most of us will endure in a lifetime. Susan was one of two children. When her brother was six and Susan was three, he died of leukemia. On that day, she began her rough ride through life.

With his traumatic death, something seemed to snap inside her parents. Either they were afraid to love their remaining child, or Susan reminded them of their trauma so much that they could not cope with the pain of her presence. They quickly distanced themselves from her as much as they could in their upper-middle-class culture. They left her with her grandmother as often as they could, and when she began school, they left her at private schools. Susan remembered always being the last child to be picked up. More often than not, her parents left her at the school until seven o'clock or later, and the school never knew what to do with this little girl who couldn't leave or with the parents who wouldn't come to get her. Soon the parents solved the problem by shipping Susan off to a boarding school.

Susan's worst memory of her parents' indifference happened while she was at the boarding school. One Thanksgiving when she was still a preteen, Susan waited for her parents to pick her up for the holidays. She was so excited that she stood outside, packed and ready to go, when her parents drove up in a full car, a six-passenger car with six adults inside it. "Where," she thought, "will I ride?" She never forgot what happened next. Her mother got out of the car, walked over to her, and handed her a hundred-dollar bill.

"Honey," her mother said, "I'm sorry, but we can't take you with us skiing. Here's some money. Have a nice time, okay?" Then her mother turned and got back in the car and drove away. Suddenly, everything was crystal clear—her parents didn't want her, and the boarding school was an excuse to get rid of her. From that time on, she began to have discipline problems.

When Susan turned thirteen, she moved back home from boarding school to go to an excellent Christian high school. Her parents, though, continued to act as if she weren't there. They began taking long trips and leaving her alone. One time she faked a robbery at her parents' house, hoping it would scare her mother so that she would quit her job and stay at home. It didn't work.

Desperate for love, Susan began developing friendships the only way she knew how, by giving potential friends expensive presents. She was convinced she had to do something for people to love her. Soon she had a boyfriend who kept telling her she should run away from home, and finally she did just that. Taking her bank passbook, checks, and some clothes, she naively got on a bus and left. She was sixteen.

The next several years, her story was one of brushes with the law and kindness from strangers. A manicurist she happened to meet on the day she ran away took her home and gave her a room. As kind as the manicurist was, though, she used drugs and wrote bad checks. Susan lived with her until her old high school friends in-

*No one is ever
too bad
to come in,
and no one is ever
too good to stay
away.*

vited her to a Bible study at a Christian couple's home nearby. She sat in the back of the room and listened, striking up a conversation with the other person who was sitting in the back, an older woman. The woman turned out to be the owner of the home and the hostess of the Bible study. When she heard Susan's story, she insisted the young runaway come and stay with them.

For the first time, Susan felt accepted. Slowly, she began to experience God in her life. Her parents didn't go to church because they continued to blame God for killing their son. They always sent her to Christian schools, though, because they happened to be the best schools, and there she had heard about God's love. Now she was beginning to see this love in the lives of the couple who took her in.

There was a problem, though. The couple was very rich. Susan began feeling pressure to impress them. How could she pay back their generosity? How could she keep them liking her? She would have to buy them gifts. It was the only way she knew to get love and keep it. So she called her bank, reported her checks stolen, then continued to write checks on the account. She began to bring flowers home daily to the couple, and she bought expensive outfits to keep them interested in her. By this time, she had started seeing her old boyfriend again, and she bought him expensive gifts, too. The couple, of course, became suspicious about all her money, but she responded with lies.

Her first brush with the law came quickly. The bank figured out what she was doing. They decided not to prosecute if she would seek counseling, which she did. She told a series of counselors what they wanted to hear, conning them into believing her. She was not ready to let anyone help her. She didn't trust anyone. She had become a compulsive liar, and she continued trying to buy love with hot checks.

Then Susan became pregnant. She was also arrested again, this time for stealing credit cards, and was sentenced to several months in jail and was released shortly before her baby was born. She promptly gave it up for adoption.

During it all, a part of Susan was a decent girl who wanted a relationship with the Lord, and part of her was a liar and a thief. The only way she kept her conscience at bay was by rationalizing: I have to do this to survive.

Then, finally, when she was staying with a Christian couple who had counseled her in jail, she forced herself to look honestly at her past and to tell someone else the truth. In the hospital, after extensive physical and psychological tests she was diagnosed as a manic-depressive. For the first time in her life, she was able to keep a job, relax, and begin to experience a conscience over her past.

Now she takes lithium, under medical supervision, to ensure her stability. She will take this drug for the rest of her life. She is also struggling to begin again in a new place with a new, hopeful outlook for a future full of God's healing love. More than that, though, she is struggling to be open to forgiveness because her parents now want to get in touch with her. The little girl standing with the hundred-dollar bill as her parents drove away had her life close to ruin because of their neglect. Every day Susan will struggle to keep her life balanced and whole, finding strength in the Scripture that says that God will never give her more than she can bear. The question now confronting this fragile young woman, then, is: Can she forgive?

Forgiving But Not Forgetting

"I can forgive you, but I can never forget what you've done."

Most of us have done something we are ashamed of. We may have hurt a friend. We may have said the very thing that ruined a relationship. We inadvertently may have let a secret slip, or we may have just said too much at the wrong time. Maybe, in a moment of rage, we reached out in anger and became inexcusably violent. Or maybe we sinned either in a very public way or in a secret, silent way that eats at our fragile spirit day after day.

Very few of us have not been hurt by someone else, wounded in some awful way that has left a scar that will not heal. Our spouse has been unfaithful, our daughter has run away, our father has abused us, our neighbor has snubbed us, the company to which we've given twenty-five years of our lives has fired us, a total stranger has stolen our money and our peace of mind, our parents neglected us, or perhaps we've acquired some senseless disease and we wonder if God is going to hurt us too.

Some of us also hurt ourselves. Believing we are worthless, we become self-destructive. We do unforgivable things to ourselves. We abuse drugs and alcohol and food. We search for love in all the wrong places. We act out our needs in ways harmful to ourselves and others, as Susan did. We refuse to accept ourselves as we are. Slowly, we get to the point that we hate ourselves for what we've done to our own bodies and minds and souls.

"Cry out," Isaiah wrote.

Cry out indeed. When forgiveness is not a part of our lives, our cry is one of anguish. Nothing ravages a fragile spirit more than being unforgiving or unforgiven. For with every problem, pain, and bit of suffering comes an anger that looks for someone, something to blame. We may mouth such clichés as "I can forgive you—Dad, Mom, husband, wife, son, daughter—but I can never forget what you've done." Such forgiveness doesn't conceal the cry of anguish we still feel.

We still cry out.

Double Forgiveness

"Listen, people of God, your war is over," the old prophet said. "All your sins, your wrongdoings, to yourself and to all others, are pardoned. And even more than that, the Lord is giving you double forgiveness for all Israel's sins. And it's all from the Lord's hand."

This news must have sounded incredible to the people it was first written to—people either subsisting in a ruined land or living in a foreign one.

First, the idea of no more war surely would have sounded ridiculous to a people whose lives were the direct result of war after war after war. Since David's day, Jerusalem had been a military fortress, its people constantly fighting or being fought over, struggling for the power needed to survive.

Now, Isaiah was telling them that era was over. It would never be as it was before. It was a whole new day, a whole new plan. Israel would "study war no more." This new nation God was restoring would not be about war, but about redemption and peace. The nation would be a spiritual one, not a physical one. It wouldn't need to have armies to defend its borders because it wouldn't have borders. And it must be prepared for. It would be a new day for Jerusalem without the burden of guilt. All was forgiven, wiped white as snow.

But even if the Israelites could have grasped the idea that war was finally over for them, they might still have found it hard to believe that God would forgive them so easily. They had been conquered, according to Isaiah, because of their sins. Isaiah had predicted it over and over, until they were probably sick of hearing it. And they probably didn't believe him. As I mentioned in chapter 1, they had become morally and religiously bankrupt although the country itself was prospering.

That's not to say that everyone was prospering. Greed was the flip side of prosperity. Supposedly, the wealthier Israelites were banding together to raise rents until the poor lost the land to them.

And the more extreme things got, richer and poorer, the more morality slid. From verses in Isaiah 1, we can see that widows and orphans and all kinds of oppressed countrymen were not being cared for in the smallest of ways. Drunkenness was a way of life. Prosperity is not always a good thing for a country.

Ironically enough, though, temple attendance was probably at an all-time high. But Isaiah stated loudly and clearly that the sacrifices given by these people did nothing but pain God. They were done for religion's sake, not God's. In fact, they offended him.[1]

They were so morally, socially, and religiously corrupt that Isaiah was reluctant to accept God's calling. The first six chapters of Isaiah explain just how bad they were. After all that, Isaiah described his reluctant acceptance of his call, almost as if he were explaining to the reader, "Look, this is what I am going to have to contend with! This is why I wasn't thrilled with the idea of preaching to this nation." But he did. And his refrain had become repent or be conquered.

So, ultimately, God had allowed them to be conquered. But all that was past now. Now the time was right. He was coming back, and he had forgiven his people double. Without their asking he was doing it. " 'Comfort my people,' says *your* God," the chapter begins. Wherever they were in captivity, even if they had been worshiping the gods of their captors, which slaves were forced to do, he said, "I am your God, and I am coming back and all is forgiven—not once but twice."

Sometimes forgiveness is not easy to accept. We, like the Israelites, might hear the words but don't believe the words can really be true. We can't believe the warfare of our soul could be over. *Nothing could be that easy,* we think. And we certainly can't believe that we can be forgiven *double* for all we've done.

Seventy Times Seven

Remember in the New Testament when Peter asked Jesus how many times we should forgive others?[2] I can see Peter proudly suggesting that perhaps the number should be seven times, quite generous considering that the rabbinical teaching of the time stated a man should forgive only three times. Here Peter, somewhat self-satisfied, was offering to forgive seven whole times. Surely, Jesus would be proud of his generosity.

But what did Jesus answer? "Seventy times seven." There is no end to our forgiveness, Jesus was saying.

Forgiveness is a godly, not a human action. It is only easy when we learn to take on the mind of God, free of such negative feelings as revenge and hate. Perhaps that fact is why we find it just as hard to believe that God can so easily forgive us.

Susan struggled with this concept of forgiveness for months after her parents began to contact her. At first, she would not return their calls. "Why are they interested now?" she would yell. She had every right to hate them for what they had caused her to do to herself. In all those years of her trying everything to get their attention, to feel loved and wanted, they had continued to ignore her. Then when she began to get in trouble, they still wanted little to do with her. She never once saw them while she was in jail. She had never even told them when she got pregnant and had the child in jail. Now, when she was finally pulling her life together, thinking she was free of that awful need for love from her parents, they called. And kept calling.

After six or seven calls which she would not return, her husband confronted her. "Do you think they are going to go away?"

"They always did before."

"It looks to me like they may have changed."

"Too late," she said with a sneer. Her husband grabbed her arm.

"Susan, you've come so far. Maybe to go any further you're going to have to find a way to forgive them and let it all go."

With that, she began to cry. How could she forgive them? She couldn't even forgive herself.

Forgiving Ourselves

Are you hard on yourself? One of the principles of forgiving and forgetting is this: Before we can learn to forgive others, we must learn to forgive ourselves.

The Israelites obviously needed to hear the same message. "Listen," Isaiah said. "You are forgiven." You must hear this and forgive yourselves and believe that God forgives you before you can become what God wants you to be. You must believe that God has forgiven you for turning your own way, for believing too much in your own powers and wisdom.

And the most interesting thing about this blanket forgiveness is that God didn't wait until the Israelites had tried to atone for their actions. He didn't wait until they'd asked for forgiveness or forgiven themselves for what they'd done. He forgave them in his own time— that moment—and expected them to hear and believe.

Do you think you have to be good before you can be God's? He doesn't automatically look for people with perfect records to do his work. Have you ever noticed? He often seems to be more interested in those whom logic would rule out. Moses was a murderer. Matthew was a despised tax collector. Peter was proud and often weak. Mary Magdalene was a prostitute. David was an adulterer and a murderer. Jacob was a thief. God doesn't wait for us to make ourselves clean. He cleanses us himself. "Though your sins be as scarlet, they shall be as white as snow," said Isaiah earlier in his book.[3]

He forgives us. Who do we think we are to not forgive ourselves?

Chris Knippers has done some counseling with one of the infamous Charles Manson gang. The man's name was Charles Watson, and he was one of the social outcasts under the influence of Manson, the cult leader who in the late seventies ordered his group to murder brutally a whole houseful of people, including actress Sharon Tate in the Los Angeles area.

Charles had been brought up in a somewhat religious home in Texas, but he began to drift during those hippie years. He was naive and impressionable, and when he met Charles Manson, Manson gave him drugs and was kind to him. So Watson began traveling around with him and the others who had fallen under Manson's spell.

When Chris first met Charles Watson, though, he could not believe that this man was part of one of the most heinous crimes of the century. Watson was kind, considerate, and unassuming. Chris has worked in prison with plenty of sociopaths and psychopaths who felt no guilt over their crimes. They all had hard exteriors, like robots. But Chris felt a softness in Charles Watson, and he soon found out that Watson had become a Christian.

Watson told Chris that when he first entered prison, he stayed withdrawn for a long time. Then his cellmate became a Christian through the prison ministries and soon, hearing the good news, Charles began to comprehend the horror of what he'd done.

"How can you stand to sleep at night knowing what you've done?" Chris asked Watson. "How do you handle the guilt?"

"I've just slowly been able to accept God's forgiveness," Watson answered. "I've fully experienced it. So I don't feel a lot of guilt anymore." Chris studied Watson as he said this, and he realized his freedom from guilt was much different from a sociopath's absence of guilt. Watson's had a soft quality that coincided with Watson's whole demeanor. God's forgiveness—and Charles' acceptance of that forgiveness—transformed him from the subhuman he had been under Charles Manson's influence.

The Shackles of Not Forgiving

Dr. Lewis Smedes in his excellent book, *Forgive and Forget,* speaks of the power of forgiveness for the forgiver. He believes strongly that the healthiest thing we can do for ourselves is to forgive those who have wronged us even if they don't accept our forgiveness. Why? Because it hurts us more to hold the grudge. It eats away at our insides. It becomes a monster, in effect, that can threaten to devour us. So when we learn how to forgive others, we help ourselves. As Dr. Smedes puts it: "When you forgive someone for hurting you, you perform spiritual surgery inside your soul; you cut away the wrong that was done to you so that you can heal your soul, we heal ourselves. . . . Forgiveness is love's antidote for hate."[4]

Forgiving, Dr. Smedes admits, is almost unnatural. Our natural response is to want some pleading for forgiveness from the one who hurt us. We want fairness and restitution. We focus on the other person, instead of grasping what the situation is doing to us.

But the rewards of "letting go" are seen not so much in the forgiver's relationship to others as in his or her relationship with God. To forgive is to be washed clean and to feel that cleansing. That's the secret—and the only real way to be capable of forgiving others.

The same holds true for forgiving yourself. God, said Isaiah, has doubled your forgiveness. You should feel clean and whole. The mistakes you have made have been forgiven—not a little bit, not adequately, but abundantly. Pressed down and shaken together. Once, twice, totally, completely, in every way, wrapped around, washed around, forgiven, and forgotten.

Do you believe that? If God can forgive Charles Watson, can't God forgive you?

The dynamic involved with such belief and such forgiveness is amazing in its power. And when you put it into motion you see how it is truly possible to forget as well as forgive.

You'll see, as Charles Watson did, the power of forgiveness to transform your fragile spirit.

When Susan's husband confronted her with the fact that she would never be free of the past until she had done the work of forgiveness, she knew she would have to look inward first. Just like Charles Watson, she would have to make a leap of faith to believe that God would forgive her for hurting so many people, for making the mess she had made in her mad scramble away from her neglectful parents. So with her husband, she tried it. And then over and over, she would remind herself of the fact that God meant it when he said he'd forgiven her. Now she would have to take on the mind of God and understand how to forgive herself.

It was a first step toward wholeness. And she took it. "Your Lord has forgiven you," she told herself.

What a wonderful thought. Whatever you've done, you are forgivable. Whatever others have done to you, you still have the power to release their hold on you by forgiving them and flooding your mind with the positive thoughts that foster a successful life.

Being Willing

Susan, though, still had to deal with her parents. How could she face these people? She knew God had forgiven them, just as she now knew God had forgiven her. How, even if she said the words, could she make forgiveness truly happen inside her fragile spirit?

Her story parallels the story of another person, a man named George, who was also bent and wounded by parental mistakes.

George had always had a chaotic relationship with his father. He had spent his whole life being hurt by the most important man in his life. His father was a Jekyll and Hyde in the way he treated George. As a child, George never knew when his father would go off into a fit of rage and take it out on him. Later, George went into business with his father, and his father more than once stole from the business. Each time he let his son down, George's father would try to make it up in strange ways, like buying George a car.

George understandably was angry with his father. He was able to forgive everyone else who had hurt him, but he couldn't forgive his father because he never knew when he might hurt him again. And this one negative attitude had made George self-destructive in other areas of his life, especially his relationships with other men. His anger would flare up with no warning, against anyone at any time.

He knew his flare-ups stemmed from his anger toward his father, but he had never decided to do anything about that anger. "He's the one that's hurt me!" he'd always say. "Why should I forgive him? He'll just do it again."

Finally, though, after one of his fits of rage had embarrassed him thoroughly, he decided he must take a long hard look at his father. And he began that day to see his father differently. He spent more and more time with his father, something he had always hated to do. And he noticed that his anger began to dissipate and his father's craziness began to subside. George had found a way to make forgiveness work.

What had made the difference? George allowed *time to do its work*. He decided to try giving this new attitude a try. He found it hard to forgive his father by just saying the words, so he developed his positive attitude over time. But before he could allow time to do its work, he had to be willing to allow forgiveness to begin. And that is a very big step.

The willingness to forgive is a positive force, and the moment George opened his relationship with his father to the possibility of forgiveness, he unleashed the God-like quality of forgiveness and the possibility that the grace of God could begin to work its miracle. Soon all of George's relationships grew better. He was able to get closer to people, he loosened up and became a more positive person, and even his career began to take off.

And that is what happened to Susan, too. The next time her parents called, she talked to them instead of cutting them off. She asked how they were doing. She was, after all, interested in their lives, since she had always loved them.

Over the next weeks, as she continued to talk to them on the phone, she began to understand them as adults who had never been able to overcome their tragedy as she had. *They're the ones who are weak,* she realized. *They need my help.*

Slowly she began to reach out to her parents. And slowly, ever so slowly, God gave her the strength to let go of the years of resentment. After several months, she was able to meet with her parents face to face, and she felt the miracle of forgiveness in her spirit.

As time aided the work of forgiveness, Susan's whole life changed. She was able to think about her hometown without wincing, and she could even face the people she had hurt and those who had hurt her, all because she allowed the poison of an unforgiving spirit to seep out of her system over time. The process was slow, but she and George both persisted even when their resolve was weak. The result was they could look positively toward the future and forget about the past. Their spirits had been strengthened and empowered.

Our fragile spirits need the soothing, restorative power of forgiveness. Perhaps you haven't even been aware that part of your pain has been caused by an unforgiving spirit. Look hard at yourself and at the relationships that have hurt you over the years.

Are you allowing your feelings toward pivotal people in your life to dictate how you feel right now?

Are you allowing your guilt and anger toward yourself to keep you in your own prison of hurt and suffering?

Look at yourself hard. You may find, as George and Susan did, that when you take an honest look at your own life and at your true feelings, you are responsible for whether you allow the past to dictate your future behavior.

Forgiving is a healthy exercise for strengthening your fragile spirit for all your days to come.

The voice of one crying in the wilderness:
"Prepare the way of the LORD;
Make straight in the desert
A highway for our God.
Every valley shall be exalted,
And every mountain and hill shall be made
  low;
The crooked places shall be made straight,
And the rough places smooth;
The glory of the LORD shall be revealed,
And all flesh shall see it together;
For the mouth of the LORD has spoken."

—Isaiah 40:3–5

Chapter 4

Searching for Peace

D uring a neighborhood parade, a truck, announcing services for a nearby church, had a makeshift float built on its bed and members smiling and waving to the crowd, inviting them to church. The church minister was driving. Suddenly, the truck went out of control. It careened into a crowd of parade watchers on the sidewalk and hit a pregnant woman. The woman and her unborn child died.

In 1988 hurricane Gilbert cuts a path of destruction across Jamaica and the Cayman Islands and then veered out to sea, seemed to stop, but instead circled, gathered strength, and hit the Yucatan Peninsula with all its force. It wreaked havoc on popular places such as Cozumel and Cancun, but also on unknown, squalidly poor villages like La Carbonera, where people who had little lost everything.

A young girl dies of leukemia. A hemophiliac acquires AIDS during a blood transfusion. Pointless tragedy is everywhere. Our first human reaction after such sorrow is to try to find a reason for such happenings. Nobody's fault, people say. Too often, that's the way the world seems—pointless.

Peace Is a Promise

The last thing most of us feel today is a peace. Dictionaries define peace as a state of tranquility or quiet, a freedom from civil disturbances, a state of security. In other words, peace is a quiet confidence. We want it, we long for it, we pray for it, but it's evasive. And it can not be sought and gained without effort.

How then can we find this peace? How can our valleys be exalted? How can our mountains and hills be made low? How can we look at a world where people hurt and feel any sense of tranquility at all? And how can we offer peace to others who hurt? Our spirits are so fragile that they can break easily. All we have to combat that fragility is a promise.

But oh, what a promise!

Isaiah puts it this way:

A voice cries in the wilderness: Prepare the way for the Lord. Make straight in the desert a highway for your God. Every valley will be lifted up and every mountain and hill be made low. The rough places will be made flat and the glory of the Lord will be renewed.

This is the promise of hope, of strength, of peace.

Often, when I think of Christmas, I begin to look forward to hearing that great piece of music, Handel's *Messiah*. I can hear parts of it echo in my ear all through the year as I read the Scripture passages the great composer set to heavenly music. And one of those echoes is happening right now: "Every valley shall be exalted, every hill shall be made low, the crooked straight, and the rough places plain. . . ." This passage speaks of the coming of our Lord, describing the difference he will make in the lives of the Israelites, in the lives of all who believe. Every valley—every hill—every rough place, all smoothed out, all made passable.

Try-umph
in tragedy.

In Isaiah's day, this idea of shouting good news from the mountaintop meant something very specific to Israelites. In ancient times, it was customary for kings and princes to send out messengers before them. These scouts made sure the paths were clear to travel. They removed rocks and bushes and thorns. They built bridges and widened narrow places, making smooth the path for their lord and master to come.

You can see the parallel, I'm sure. Isaiah told his readers to do all we can to change the path we are walking upon, to make it as good as we can, to have the right attitude—so we will be prepared for our Lord and Master who comes. And when he comes all the highs and lows and crooked places will be made straight again.

But when you are in a valley and you can't find your way out of its depths, how can you prepare?

That was where the minister whose truck killed the woman found himself. He of all people should have been able to handle the tragedy around him.

But how could he? Because of his truck, two lives were snuffed out, one who had not even had a chance at life. He kept seeing the horrified faces of the bystanders who stood three or four deep on parade route, almost frozen as they watched his truck veer toward them. He could hear the float decorations falling off the back of the truck and the people jumping off. All but one of the people was able to break the frozen spell and get out of his way—all but the woman and her unborn child. After hitting her, his out-of-control truck rammed into a store front. Bleeding from a gash in his head, he stumbled back to the woman and lay down and cried until his family helped him to the hospital.

Then, he found himself in a valley with no peace. Weeks passed, and still no peace.

A Shaft of Light

When you are in the valleys, it's often difficult to see the sun. In a place called Petra in Jordan, you can enter the city only one way, through a gorge. The gorge is so narrow that you can actually touch both sides of the cliff. And the cliffs go straight up for about two hundred feet. It's one of the most incredible places I've ever seen.

I took a donkey through that gorge for a mile and a half to visit the ancient city of Petra, a town that is literally carved out of the side of the rock. Over fifteen thousand people lived there during biblical days, but even then the only way to get there was through that gorge.

We journeyed through that gorge for about an hour, and during that whole hour only for a moment—just a moment—did a shaft of light break through and hit me. But it was there. And it did hit me.

In the Darkest Place

When I think of that shaft of light, I think of Jennifer Carter.

Jennifer Carter is an extraordinary diver. She was part of the film crew who made the two-and-a-half-mile dive down to the wreck of the *Titanic* and the first woman ever to go down there.

As you might expect, the dive itself was quite dangerous. She had to have complete faith in the module she would be riding for two hours straight down. The slightest hairline crack anywhere on the small sub module would cause her and all aboard to be crushed by the enormous pressure building as they dropped a hundred feet a minute to the bottom of the ocean floor. The slightest problem would mean death.

In her explanation of her sensations as the submarine-type module went deeper and deeper in the water, she explained that the water turned from green to gray, then to a black darker than night. To conserve power, the module was not using any lights, so beyond a faint red glow of monitors on board there was only the blackness of the porthole. With nothing to see, she said there was no falling sensation even though she was moving at a hundred feet a minute. Suddenly, something outside the porthole made her gasp. Six inches from her face on the other side of the porthole a streak of light sped upward and then vanished. It happened again and again. She finally realized that these ghost streaks were bioluminescent sea creatures, glowing all by themselves in the eternal night of ocean.

There was life, even there. Life went on in the blackest of black places on planet Earth. More than that, *because* of that deep darkness, the life had its own inner light. The Creator was at work even there, and what a wonderful symbol those fantastic creatures are for us. God is there. In the blackest black, the darkest depths of despair, light gleams. God's presence is there.

Regardless of how deep and how narrow the valleys are, the light can find its way to you. Regardless of the anguish that you feel—in the wilderness of your life, in the valleys, in the rough places, wherever you are—there is the Lord. And with him comes his peace.

Why then is it so hard for us to know that peace? Prepare, Isaiah says. Perhaps peace is a thing to prepare for. Perhaps we need to be available for it. The pain of this world can harden us to this sort of peace. It may be there, and we may miss it because we aren't prepared to recognize it and accept it.

Knowing Isn't Always Doing

Have you ever known the right thing to do, yet felt something inside that made you refuse to do it?

Before you shake your head, think of that greasy hamburger and french fries you probably had for lunch or that cigarette you had this morning. We all do things we know we shouldn't do.

Here in California, speeding is a way of life. The freeways are full of people trying to get places, and everyone seems to be going there as fast as possible. A joke about an L.A. freeway is that it's the only place that the traffic is bumper to bumper at eighty miles an hour.

It's not as if we don't have speed limits. We do. And it's not as if we don't know we shouldn't be driving that fast because we know the reasons we shouldn't—safety, conservation of gas. Even though it's almost unsafe *not* to speed when everyone around you is, speeding is still against the law. The highway patrol's answer to this dilemma seems to be that since almost everyone is speeding, it will randomly stop as many drivers as possible.

Having just visited the dentist, I am also thinking

about something I rarely do but that I know I should do every day—flossing. Now who among us enjoys tooth flossing? But what dentist doesn't tell us that it could make the difference between a good checkup and a bad one?

Most of us will readily admit that we do such things as speed, smoke, eat foods that aren't good for us, forget to floss. Most of us yell at our children even as a voice inside us tells us we are doing exactly what we vowed we'd never do. Most of us say the very things we should not say to our spouses, even as we know we are doing it. We readily admit that we shouldn't. It's easy enough to do that. The next step is the one that's tough—to actually make the commitment to change.

I know a psychologist who is an "ACA," an adult child of an alcoholic. In the last few years, psychology has realized that the family members of an alcoholic suffer just as much as and perhaps more, in some ways, than the alcoholic. The children of alcoholics grow up learning many wrong lessons about how to relate to others and carry behavioral scars all through their lives and relationships. Doug is an ACA. He is also a bright, sensitive young counselor who has helped scores of people sort out their own problems, many alcohol related.

He will tell you that one of the patterns of an ACA is unwittingly choosing an alcoholic for a mate and then repeating the patterns he or she saw between his own parents. Doug can tell you about this pattern and show you how it is destructive, but he has had a hard time not enacting this very pattern in his own life.

Over and over, Doug found himself doing the very

thing he knew not to do. At first, he was meeting women in bars, only to find out later that each one had a drinking problem. Finally he noticed that the pattern was repeating itself so much that he quit going to bars, blaming the situation on the environment he was searching in.

During the next few years, though, nothing changed but the environment in which he would meet such women. He found himself involved with one woman after another, ones he met at charity functions or even church, and one by one, he learned that each had a drinking problem. During each relationship, he was certain that this woman could change, that he could change her, even though as a psychologist he knew better. Each woman, he argued with himself, had wonderful qualities except for the drinking problem. How could he end the relationship? Each new relationship, though, turned out the same way—fighting over her drinking problem.

Doug kept telling himself, "Hey, I'm a Christian. I'm a psychologist. I'm an adult child of an alcoholic. I know better. Why do I keep putting myself into the same situation over and over again?" The only answer he could give was that unconsciously he was acting out deeply embedded childhood responses that kept him doing the very things his head and all his degrees told him were self-defeating.

The very thing that he did not want to do, Doug kept doing. It wasn't as if Doug were spiritually weak. Even the apostle Paul, that strongest of the strong Christians, had trouble with the very same feelings. I don't know what I'm doing, he said, because what I want to do I don't do, but instead I do what I hate.[1]

Doesn't that sound familiar?

Doug and the apostle Paul both admit to struggling, but in going one step further, they show their spiritual strength. They commit to change. Most people never make that commitment. A hardness of spirit keeps us from such a commitment. To prepare that sort of hard spirit for peace is quite a job, and many people never undertake it.

God Never Gives Up

Not too long ago, I was reading a copy of *Guideposts,* Norman Vincent Peale's inspiring magazine. In the July 1988 issue there is a story about a young man whose spirit was hardened by a pointless tragedy and who allowed his life to be ruined by the resulting guilt. Yet, through a tough old man, he was slowly prepared for the peace of the Lord.[2]

The young man's name was Fred LeFever. When he was twelve, he talked his dad into going on a camping trip along with a friend and the friend's father, even though Fred's father did not want to go due to back problems. But Fred begged his father, and his father didn't want to disappoint him. So they both went.

After they settled into the friend's cabin, the two dads took a boat and headed across the river for groceries. A storm blew up, and all night long the two boys waited for their fathers to come back. They didn't. They had both drowned.

Fred was devastated. He felt he had killed his father by talking him into going on the camping trip. The guilt turned ugly by the time he was a teenager. He quickly got into drugs and trouble. The army didn't help. He was sent home for drug dealing. He went from one hospital to another trying to kick his habit, but to no avail. Soon he forged a check, then was picked up for drug possession, and was finally sent to a maximum security prison.

His mother kept telling him he was loved, but Fred wouldn't believe it. Out of prison on a work release at age twenty-one, Fred found that there was never enough money to feed his addiction, so he bought a water pistol and managed to pull off a couple of robberies. Even though he was scared, he walked into the Ideal Pharmacy in Seattle, pointed his toy gun at the old pharmacist behind the counter, and looked at the man who would start the change in his life.

The old man looked at the gun, looked at Fred, then shook his head. He walked around the counter and up to Fred. He told Fred he wasn't scared of him and that he had been shot before. Then he put his hand on Fred's shoulder and began sharing Christ with him. Fred ran out the door.

Soon Fred was caught and the druggist's description helped send Fred back to prison. But the strangest thing happened. The druggist inquired about Fred and began to write him. He wrote Fred that he had been shot in the eye by other robbers and had kept up with them in prison too. With his letters, he began to send Fred religious pamphlets.

But Fred would have nothing to do with religion. He ignored the pamphlets. Ten years went by, and he left jail. Within only a short time, though, he was back in prison, and there, in his cell, he began thinking that maybe he should just end it all. But he also thought of the old pharmacist, who was dead by then and realized that maybe he should have listened. Thinking about that old man and his own life, Fred cried out to Jesus, if there was a Jesus, he said, for help. The strangest sense of peace fell over him. *Maybe there is a Jesus,* he thought.

Then two weeks later, one of the prison officers told him that a couple in his church had read about him and wanted to write him. The woman was the daughter of that crusty old pharmacist. And soon the whole family had taken him on as their special project, especially the youngest daughter, Kim. Finally, Fred was slowly coming to grips with what guilt had done to him.

But the most fantastic part of the story was still to come. Kim fell in love with Fred, and Fred, who had been telling everyone he was innocent of the robberies that sent him to jail, confessed his guilt. With that, Kim insisted they get married. They were married in the prison chapel, neither knowing if Fred would spend the rest of his life in jail.

Then suddenly a state supreme court ruled that his earlier trial had erred, and he was to have a retrial. Through a court drama straight out of a Perry Mason script, Fred and all the people who now loved him, his own family and the druggist's family—both groups who had never given up on Fred—stood in front of the judge who would decide Fred's fate for the next thirty years. The judge decided to put Fred on probation and ordered him to make restitution to the places he had robbed. Today, Fred is studying to be a prison chaplain.

The light continued to search for Fred, even when he kept moving back into the dark corners. Finally it found him. The light can find you, too. That's Isaiah's word. Prepare the way of the Lord, and he will find you. Prepare yourself for the One who can bring peace and assurance and direction. This is the prophecy Isaiah is best known for, and it's all about the peace that is on its way in the form of the Messiah, the peace that comes from a new understanding available through Jesus Christ.

Do you believe he's trying to find you? It's hard in the midst of pain and problems to believe that the God of the universe cares at all.

Isaiah said it first: "All flesh shall see it together." Then in the New Testament, Luke said it: "All flesh shall see the salvation of God."[3]

No matter where you have been, no matter where you have gone, no matter where you will be going, God's salvation is here. His love, his mercy, and his grace abound beyond our wildest comprehensions, and his arms are wide open, ready to encompass and draw you unto him. You are his. He is yours.

It will happen. Peace. We can find it through Christ now if we will look for him, even in our tough times.

Robert Wise, pastor of Our Lord's Community Church in Oklahoma City and former president of the First Reformed Church of America, is writing a book, *When the Night Is Too Long*. In it, he proposes that we often ask the wrong questions during our tough times. We ask, "Where is God when disaster strikes?" and usher in an enemy of the soul called despair.

"The issue is not 'where,'" Wise suggests, "but can I recognize how God is present to me right now?" We must learn, he says, to develop an inner perception that recognizes what our sensory system cannot record.

How do we do this? Wise suggests listening to Handel's *Messiah,* to some of the words we are considering in this book. He suggests the beauty of nature. When he lived in California, he enjoyed, as I do, strolling along the beaches, which always seemed to heighten his sense of God's presence.

A final sign of God in the midst of tragedy, he suggests, is the place where suffering and goodness meet: "We are often surprised by how much of the presence of God arises out of the mix. Caring people can turn emptiness into fullness."

Often that involves action. Strength for your fragile spirit is there. But it's not something that happens without your effort.

Acting on Peace

Peace is much like comfort. To find peace, often you must act. Perhaps it isn't acting on the problems of your life; perhaps it has nothing to do with what is going on in your own life. It could be reaching out to someone else in need. But the very act of doing something outside yourself can actually be a catalyst for change and peace in your life.

Let me tell you what happened at our church when I decided to see what we could do to help a small Mexican town. Right after hurricane Gilbert finished its reign of destruction in the Caribbean, photos showed up in our local papers. During this time, our church was in the most severe financial crunch it had ever faced. Bills were not being paid. It was a negative, troublesome time.

I don't subscribe to the local paper, but for some reason, it was in my driveway the morning after the hurricane hit the mainland of Mexico. I picked it up and saw on the front page a photo of a man standing in front of what used to be his little house in a small Mexican coastal town called La Carbonera. At the time, I didn't know that La Carbonera was located about 150 miles south of Brownsville, Texas, two thousand miles from my home. This village took the full force of the storm.

So there I was, in my nice home, sitting at my desk in my study, looking at this photo of a man standing in the rubble of his house. Quite nonchalantly I mentioned to my wife, Donna, "I wish I could do something to help this man."

"Why don't you?" she asked.

Those words hit hard and deep. "If I really wanted to, I probably could do *something* to help."

So I began thinking how I might. I decided that if I was serious I would have to fly down there so I could find out what the victims' specific needs were. Then perhaps I could raise some money to help. So I checked the flights.

The closest flight would take me 150 miles from La Carbonera. And once there, I would have no guarantee of finding a taxi or a car to rent in order to get to the village. The only chance I had of getting there would be by way of a private airplane. So I called different people who had planes, hoping they might fly me there. My plan was to leave early in the morning, land at the airport in La Carbonera, take pictures, talk to the people to find out their needs, get back on the plane, and return to San Juan Capistrano to start collecting the things they needed. It was an exhausting search, which led me to the Missionary Aviation Fellowship, an organization that supplies planes for missionaries. They knew someone who would fly me to La Carbonera if I'd pay for the fuel. The man's name was Bill Vanderpole.

I called Bill, and by 10:30 that night, I had set up the flight. Believe it or not, the following morning, I was flying in a twin engine Apache to a place I wasn't even quite sure where it was. Bill informed me that we would not arrive until the next day. That took me by surprise. What I thought I could do in one day would take me three. After two days in a small plane, going through thunderstorms and dealing with extremely cold temperatures, we were able to fly over La Carbonera.

From the air we could see boats that had been picked up and thrown in the middle of marshes two or three miles inland. Most of the men had made their livelihood with those boats. If they ever found the boats, they would never be able to get them back to the shore through the dense foliage. And the only airstrip in La Carbonera was too destroyed even for this bush plane to land. So we had to land 35 miles away in a resort which was itself severely damaged.

That turned out to be a blessing—every burden is a blessing! The owner of the resort informed us we would not be able to go to the village without clearance from the provincial president, whose office was located 30 miles in the opposite direction from La Carbonera. Thanks to the resort owner, we were ushered into the president's office where we shared our desire to help. The president not only gave us permission to go to La Carbonera but also gave us a truck and a driver to get us there safely. Finally, thirty-two hours after leaving Southern California, we arrived at La Carbonera.

The villagers' homes before the hurricane had consisted of dirt floors, tar paper, minimal framing, and tin. The homes had had no plumbing, no heat, no electricity. Their homes had literally blown away. I had expected thirty to forty homes to be in shambles. But the whole village was gone. I could only guess where the houses had stood because they had all been built over dirt floors. As I stood in the middle of what had once been a house, the only remains were the four holes in the ground left by the corner posts.

None of the villagers had any money or insurance, so they had no means to rebuild their village. The people were sleeping out in the open. The possessions they had been able to save were sitting under trees and on the beach. Yet I felt a sense of peace coming from the villagers. I think they could see that something was happening. The Red Cross had been dropping food and water for several days, and others like me were visiting. They had hope that things would be okay.

I took pictures and then flew back home. I did some research and found out it would cost about four hundred to five hundred dollars to rebuild each home. There were six hundred homes in the village, so the total cost would be about two hundred thousand dollars.

I came up with a challenge for my church. My congregation, already facing financial difficulty, came up with a generous amount, and as I sought other sources of gifts, many were helpful. I knew I had to find an organization that had means and skills so that the funds would go to the right people. World Vision agreed they would accept all the funds I could raise and would add any other funds necessary to complete the project. I was able to raise over twenty thousand dollars from our church and other sources. World Vision did the rest.

But in the meantime, our financial need at the church had not gone away. With all the scandals rocking televangelism at the time, people weren't giving as much. I believe that many people had lost some of their faith in the institution of the church, and our financial crisis was a result. We were thirty-two thousand dollars behind in our budget.

With the La Carbonera project, though, the spirit of the congregation turned around. Even though we needed money to meet our own needs, we decided to reach out to others in greater need. Soon we weren't as upset about ourselves. Oh, many were still worried and had to fight being negative, but we couldn't ignore how much we had been blessed. In helping others, we had a chance to rely on God to change our attitudes and thereby lift our burden. We began to believe that God would help us find a way to meet our needs as we had helped others.

That, I'm excited to say, is exactly what happened. God met our need—in a most unusual way.

Exactly a Tithe

Mark and Carol Doyle are members of our congregation. One Sunday, Mark came up to me before the church service and said he wanted to donate some money to the church and wondered if I could suggest a need his money might fill. I considered telling him about what we had been doing at La Carbonera, but I decided this time I needed to tell about our thirty-two-thousand-dollar debt problem.

And so I explained to him that we needed every penny we could get to pay our bills. Somehow I got the impression that Mark wanted to give a thousand dollars or so, and I suggested that if he was thinking about giving, we would certainly appreciate help with our debt.

Mark just shook his head and walked off. Then after church, he and his wife walked up and handed me a check. I thanked them and folded the check without looking at it. Carol said, "Robert, maybe you ought to look at the check."

Well, I didn't want to gawk at the check with Mark and Carol standing there, so I just said, "No, that's okay. Mark already told me he wanted to give a thousand dollars toward retiring the church's debts, and we really thank you."

But she persisted. "I think you ought to look at the check." I didn't want to insult her, so I opened up the check. Written on the check was the amount of thirty-two thousand dollars, the largest unsolicited gift our church had ever received. Mark said, "Well, we had a little windfall, and we thought we'd share it."

I went home praising God, but my curiosity got the better of me. I called Mark that night and stammered, "Uh, Mark, how did you . . . ? What kind of business did you say you were in?"

I heard a laugh on the other end, and then he said, "Well, Robert, I've got to tell you. I know this sounds crazy, but I said if I ever won any money in the lottery, I would tithe. I bought a ticket the other day for the California lottery, and I won. And then at church, when you told me how much the church was in debt, well, I couldn't believe it. It was exactly a tenth of what I had won."

Let me add that I have never bought a lottery ticket and never intend to, but I'm glad that God works, even if it is in mysterious ways.

The moment we began helping others was the moment that we released the power that God gives us— the peace that can handle any hurt, any pain, any suffering, any problem.

Peace in Action

And that is also what happened to the minister who accidentally killed the woman during the parade. After weeks of trying to forgive himself, he still could not forget the sight of the woman he'd killed. He knew, though, that he must force himself to go back to work even if he would only be going through the motions. He knew God had forgiven him, and his ministry could not wait while he found his personal peace.

One of the church's ministries was with an orphanage only two blocks away, and he and a group were slated to go that afternoon. He had always enjoyed his church's ministry of visiting and befriending the children. But during this trip, he felt different. He saw all these children with no parents, through the parents' death or disappearance. And then, as he began to make a shy little eight-year-old girl laugh, he felt a chemical change inside of him. Here, while helping a little girl know the joy of laughing, he felt peaceful. In the weeks ahead, he found himself going more and more to the orphanage to minister but also to have his fragile spirit ministered to.

God's Power Is There

The shaft of light is always there. Good things can happen. Good things will happen as we make ourselves available to God. Whatever the problem, God's miraculous power can move through it if we do our best, if we believe. The solutions and the peace are there.

We've been reminded of that truth last year with *The Hour of Power,* and we learned the same lesson at God's feet. One of the major stations was WOR of Chicago. Its satellite transmits all through the nation, reaching 10 percent of the whole *Hour of Power* audience. Last year, WOR decided that they were going to drop not only *The Hour of Power* but all religious broadcasting from the station, and they would not sell us the time for any amount. Period. Overnight, 10 percent of our audience was gone. We began to question the future of *The Hour of Power.* What would happen? Were other television stations going to move in this same direction? Would the only possibility for survival be to buy stations so that we could control the availability of time?

We looked into buying stations and found the cost so absurd that it was impossible even to dream of such an option. What could we do? We could pray for possibilities that God might open.

Then the possibility came. Media tycoon Rupert

Murdoch had recently launched a new satellite called Sky Channel. It will hover over Europe and beam down from Norway all the way to Greece. Already, 275 television stations have agreed to pick up this satellite transmission and broadcast it. The number of people that will be able to pick up Sky Network from Murdoch's satellite is estimated to be over thirty-two million.

Here is the miracle. If Sky Channel had offered to sell us time on the transmission, we wouldn't have been able to afford it. But they are giving *The Hour of Power* one hour every week *free*.

When the people of God say, "Okay, Lord, you and I can do it together," things can change. You can realize your full potential. Learning about God's peace can flood your soul in the midst of hardship and make things new.

What is your problem? What is making your spirit fragile? God's peace has been promised to us. His light can find us if we allow it to. Consider today how the peace of God can find you as you seek to find it—by acting, helping, doing, in whatever mysterious ways God opens to you.

If you don't think it will make a difference in your problems, my suggestion is, "Try it; you'll like it." And you'll never regret it. You will be wonderfully surprised as the light shaft hits you.

Oh Zion,
You who bring good tidings,
Get up into the high mountain;
Oh Jerusalem,
You who bring good tidings,
Lift up your voice with strength,
Lift it up, be not afraid;
Say to the cities of Judah,
"Behold your God!"

Behold the Lord comes with a strong hand,
And His arm shall rule for Him. . . .
He will feed His flock like a shepherd;
He will gather the lambs with His arm,
And carry them in His bosom,
And gently lead those who are with young.

—Isaiah 40:9–11

Chapter 5

Can You Hear the News?

When my wife, Donna, was carrying our youngest child, she was always saying she was hot. The longer she carried the baby, the hotter she seemed to get. She called it her little hot water bottle. She talked about it all the time, as she sweated profusely. We were constantly changing the temperature in the house and in the car. Day after day she'd say, "Boy, I'm hot. Boy, it's warm in here. Robert," she'd say, "what am I going to do?"

I'm only human. So finally I said, "Honey, I heard you the first time you mentioned you were hot. I heard you the second time you mentioned it. I heard you the third time you said it. I have a good idea. Why don't you tell me when you are not hot?"

My wife, being the good sport she is, didn't get mad. Instead, she didn't say a word. When she was hot, she just turned up the air conditioner full blast at home or in the car, and we'd all put on sweaters or turn the vents toward her without a word being said. Finally, one night, she came up to me at home and said, "Robert."

"Yes, Donna?"

"I am feeling quite cool right now. I just thought you'd like to know."

Ah, the bearer of good news. She's always welcome. Aren't we all like that?

From the Mountaintop

Bearers of good news are welcomed people. They are fun to live with and be around. They are invited in for a cup of coffee, given big tips, asked back again, and offered the microphone.

How do you feel when you have good news? Don't you want to run to the mountaintop, to go out in the street and stop people and say, "Wow! I've got good news!"

In Isaiah's day, this idea of shouting good news from the mountaintop meant something very specific to Israelites.

In Israel, there is a mountain range called the Judean mountains. The ancient city of Jerusalem actually sits on top of one of these mountains, Mount Zion, 2,443 feet above sea level. If you were to go into Jerusalem and look for Mount Zion, you'd probably expect a mountain peak like the Prudential rock or the like. The fact is these are more like foothills, but they were still the highest around.

Jerusalem is built into the side of this mountain. On top of the mountain is the temple area. Then lower down the mountain is the rest of the city, built near the springs.

Of course there was method in this madness. The Israelites knew that their enemies using ancient warfare techniques would try to starve them out; then if they couldn't starve them, they would cut off their water supply. If that didn't work, they would storm the walls and that would mean quite a bit of bloodshed.

So what did those crafty Israelites do? They set Jeru-

The deeper the valley, the harder it is to see the sun.

salem close to the pinnacle of the hill for the view of approaching armies, built down the mountain encompassing the spring to protect it, and then finally allowed for a large area inside the city to grow enough crops to survive a siege. They reserved the highest point on Mount Zion for their temple.

So if someone wanted to tell everyone in Jerusalem a topic of good news, he'd go up on top of Mount Zion. From there all the people in the courtyards and the springs and the fields below could hear the good news.

Pass It On

What then is this good news? This message may be one of the most important points anyone can hear. Isaiah is saying, "Hey, I've got great news for you. There *is* good news. You all have the good news. Your God is here. *Your God is in control.* Pass it on."

We should be shouting it from the rooftops. We should be as excited as Isaiah was about the news: Here is your God. He will come with might! He will gather us up in his arms!

Now that's good news in anybody's language. Lift it up! Don't be afraid! Unfortunately Christians are often too timid to share this belief with others.

Chris Knippers tells a story that happened to him in the first few years of his career—a story of good news that changed not only the hearer's life, but also his own. It's an incredible story, the kind that sounds as if it were taken from a movie.

One normal day, a woman came to Chris to begin counseling. From all appearances, she was an average housewife, but there was nothing average about the amazing story she unfolded. As Chris listened, she told how she and her husband moved from New York to Southern California to start a business, raise their son, and get away from her husband's family. That's the way her husband had always explained the move although she had never been around his family enough to see what about them upset her husband. The move to California was a good one, though. His business prospered and so, she thought, did their marriage.

Then one night her husband told her that he needed to go back to New York to visit his family and he wanted to take their son for a couple of weeks. She knew that he'd been talking on the phone quite a bit with his family, so she didn't think much about it and bade them goodbye.

After two weeks, her son and husband did not come back. Two months passed, and they did not come back. She tried to contact them, but could never find them. Then after three months, her husband called her and told her that he was not ever coming back and neither was their son.

Only then did he tell her that his family was *the* family—they were in organized crime. They had threatened him with death if he did not return and bring his son with him. He had no choice, he told his wife, and she had no choice, either. She was not to try to contact him or their son, or he couldn't be responsible for what might happen to her. Her son would be under constant watch. She would never see him again.

That had been several weeks before she came to see Chris, and she had not slept a moment since. She had become physically sick from the worry and depressed beyond endurance.

Listening to this woman's terrifying story, Chris was at a loss. She'd had what she thought was an idyllic marriage, an idyllic life, and suddenly the whole world had gone sour in soap opera dimensions. How could she fight that? Chris didn't know, and he also had no idea what he could do to help her.

Chris tried every professional response he knew to console the woman. He did everything by the book. But the book didn't cover a story such as this. So Chris quietly did something that he had done many times before in situations for which he had no answers. He prayed.

God, I don't have any words for this woman, he prayed silently. *Help me help her.* The answer he received shocked even Chris.

With the next breath, Chris began telling her things he'd never thought of before. As the words came out, he was hearing them for the first time—and they were preposterous. "Don't worry, your son is fine," he told the woman. "Sometime between Thanksgiving and Christmas, you'll have your son back." And as he talked, Chris was thinking, *Where are these words coming from? This is so unethical. I'm giving false hope to this woman.*

The woman stared at Chris. "What? How could that happen?"

Chris didn't know, until he opened his mouth, and said, "You'll get a call from LAX [Los Angeles International Airport] to come pick him up."

The woman wanted so desperately to believe him

that she didn't scoff. She just stared at him wide-eyed for a moment. Then she said, "But they're watching him all the time. How can that happen?"

Chris answered, "I'm not sure, but I think there will be a moment he won't be guarded and he will get to a phone. He'll call an airline and tell them his situation and they'll send a taxi for him. He'll sneak out, and they'll fly him out here, and you'll pay the airline back." *What?* Chris was thinking as he was saying all this. *Where was all this coming from?*

The woman never doubted Chris for a moment. She thanked him and left. "I'll keep in touch," she said.

Chris thought, *When it doesn't happen, she'll get in touch, all right. I'm probably going to get sued for telling such crazy things to this poor woman.* He still had no idea where the statements had come from or why he had said what he did.

Weeks passed, and Chris didn't hear from the woman. Then several weeks after Christmas, she approached him at church. He hadn't recognized her at first. She looked radiant, and standing there beside her was her son. "It happened exactly as you said it would," she said. "After you told me, I went home and slept every night. I knew it would happen just as you said, and it did. I can't thank you enough."

After the woman left, Chris had to sit down. The woman had believed in words that Chris himself hadn't believed. He had to think this through. Something extraordinary had happened to both of them.

That encounter of extremely good news didn't just change the woman's life. Chris still feels its impact today. It changed his professional habits as well as his personal understanding of God's influence in the most impossible situations. He began to rely more on the sort of prayer he offered during his session with that woman. "God, I know you are in control of this situation," he prayed. "Show me what I can do or say to help this person." He began relying more on what came into his mind after such prayers. And to this day, he uses psychology in tandem with the insight he receives in response to prayer.

The good news that God is in control transforms the bearer just as much as it transforms the listener, and Chris' effective counseling, which has helped many others besides the woman whose husband left her, shows how God can and will use those of us who are willing to risk telling the good news.

Who's in Control?

The idea that God is in control seems to be one which anyone, especially Israelites, would be deliriously happy to hear and eager to believe.

That was not exactly the case in Isaiah's day. And we know it not to be the case with many of us today either. Picture the exiled Jews finally adjusting, surviving in a new land. Perhaps they just wanted to be left alone. They were tired of dreams and content to have the little they had eked out in a new land. In Babylon, many of the Jews didn't have it so bad, especially those who were less devout. They'd established themselves and been given freedoms—houses, land, farms, businesses.

Beyond these facts, from what they could see, their captors were still in control and awesomely powerful.

They had already lost once. If they weren't going to fight anymore, how could they ever return? It may have been almost impossible for these weary people to envision what God had in mind.

First, God wanted them to reunite spiritually. From the beginning of Isaiah's writing, when God said comfort my people, he wanted both the Northern and Southern Kingdoms, wherever they were scattered, to reach out to each other and become united again, God's kingdom, without borders or armies. Then, he wanted them to leave the rest up to him. The past was finished. This would be a whole new beginning. Many wouldn't be able to understand and embrace the difference.

Sometimes, more than we'd care to admit, we want the leading of God to make sense before we step out in faith and accept it. The Israelites were no different. They wanted proof.

Interestingly enough, the Israelites did have proof, centuries of it. If they didn't want to go all the way back to God's benevolent and unflagging care during the Exodus and wilderness wanderings—or through the miracles of Joshua conquering Jericho with a bugle and crumbling walls, or a myriad of others through David's reign—they could just glance back at the times they had listened to Isaiah.

During one of the many Assyrian sieges, when Assyria had laid waste to most of the countryside and was seriously threatening Jerusalem for the first time, King Hezekiah did all he could to make a pact with the invaders, but the Assyrian leader laughed at him. The leader even stood and taunted them to pray to their God for help. He shouted at the embattled Hebrews that they were stupid to think that their God could stop him.

With this, King Hezekiah, all out of ideas, finally went to Isaiah and pleaded for him to intercede for Jerusalem. God heard the plea, and the next morning the Israelites awoke to see 185,000 Assyrian soldiers lying dead.[1]

But the Israelites went back to their old ways and now found themselves dispersed and perhaps more than a bit hesitant to listen to Isaiah.

We know the rest of the story. Isaiah wrote in the chapters following Isaiah 40 how God would show his control by choosing a foreign ruler, Cyrus of Persia, to overrun Babylon and then allow the exiles to go home. As he has always been, as he still is, God was in control.

He keeps planning, and he keeps caring, waiting for us to choose to follow his lead.

Look at the rest of this chapter's Scripture if you doubt that God, the source of the good news, is going to care for you.

"Behold the Lord comes with a strong hand," wrote Isaiah. "He will feed his flock like a shepherd . . . and gently lead those who are with young." Strong but gentle. Both words are used. That is a wonderful word picture of how the God of the universe cares for us, his creation, his children. He will shelter us with his strength and nurture us with a shepherd's love. God cares. He's in control. That's the good news.

Yet most of the time we act like we can't hear that good news. Why?

Our deafness is usually due to a potent thing called pain.

Pain's Loud Refrain

Not too long ago, I was doing a small bit of carpentering. Considering that I tend to be the all-thumbs kind of fix-it guy, it might not surprise you that I hit my thumb instead of a nail. I was whacking away on a board, the nail head broke off and moved, and my next whack came down on my thumb.

Instantly, I could see the blood coming up under the nail and could feel the throbbing under the skin. For the next few minutes, the house could have burned down, an earthquake could have jarred the neighborhood, police cars could have roared by with sirens wailing, a nuclear bomb could have landed next door—I would not have noticed. In fact, somebody could have driven up and handed me a check for a million dollars, and believe it or not, at that moment I would not have cared a bit. All I cared about, all I could think of was that thumb.

Although I could not do a thing about my thumb, that didn't keep me from being deaf to the rest of the world. I couldn't hear a thing but the silent throbbing of my thumb because of a loud thing called pain.

That's what pain will do. Good news or bad, pain will dull it. All you can hear over and over and over is the pain's loud refrain.

But who doesn't have pain in their lives?

Can You Hear the Good News?

Lori Yoder, a friend of ours, grew up one of six children in a home with alcoholic parents. One of her earliest memories is of her Dad smelling of beer. Because of a heart condition, he didn't work, so he had more time to drink. He made their home a hell on earth, beating up Lori's mother, openly having a mistress, sexually abusing his daughters.

All this took a toll on Lori's mother. She also drank and she was constantly abusing drugs, one called "speed" in particular. Drugs and alcohol were always there for the taking, for the children as well as parents. One of her older sisters had to be institutionalized at age fifteen, because of the abuse at home.

Lori remembers not feeling safe until she started first grade where she found kindly parental figures and a stable environment for part of her day. Unfortunately, the school was closed down when she entered the third grade, so she was sent to a strict, formidable Catholic school. Lori couldn't handle that. From that point on, she was afraid of people to the point of feeling physical pain whenever she touched or was touched. Brushing against other students in the hall hurt her body.

Then, when Lori was twelve, her father died, and Lori did not mourn a minute. She was glad. For a while her home life calmed down. Then her mother began throwing wild parties, at times even trying to pick up her daughters' boyfriends. Lori began to use speed and alcohol at the tender age of twelve. She enjoyed both, she remembers, because they allowed her to not feel the pain for short periods of time. But the pain always returned with the clearing of her head. She couldn't escape its loud refrain for long.

By the time Lori had finished high school, she had learned some survival methods. She decided that she could take care of herself and would never ask for help. Only when she was forced would she make even the slightest connection with anyone. She never thought about God, and she certainly didn't feel him. All she remembered was being taught about devils and sin and guilt, not once hearing the word "love" in context with "God."

The first close friend she made was a boy who was friendly to her. She moved in with him and locked into him exclusively. He was her best friend, her only friend, and he made her feel safe. Here was a person she could rely on. She could hide from her past and her pain with him.

But he was not content hiding away with Lori. He wanted to have his friends over. He wanted to go places and do things. Lori began to feel trapped. She had no choice. She had to be around his friends, and the only way she could cope with all those people was to drink. She drank heavily, but, as she put it, she was a "happy drunk," always seemingly in control. Then she discovered her boyfriend was cheating on her. The one she had relied on let her down. Through the pain, though, she learned how to fake it.

Slowly, as she grew older she began to consider that perhaps there was something wrong with her. The pain had kept her deaf long enough, she decided. She started back to school to try to find answers, to try to figure out herself and her family.

As she began her look inward, the pain did not immediately let go. She was beginning for the first time to feel the love of God, to begin to hear his call past her pain, but at this point, all she could do was strain to hear it. She married and had children, but she was still leaning on alcohol to dull the ache of all the childhood trauma. Although she was scared for her children that the past would repeat itself, she was an alcoholic and could not stop the drinking.

Often, the memories of abuse were so strong they made her want to die. The only thing that kept her from suicide was her children and, she realizes now, that faint call of God she was beginning to hear. She had to find something to numb the hole inside her, to ease her separateness from other people, and looking back, the separateness from God, too. Still, she would not allow herself to ask God for help because the childhood lessons still told her to rely on no one, no one at all.

Then one by one her sisters and brothers, who had all gone their separate ways as soon as they could, began to surface in her life. For the first time, she realized that they had all gone out of their way to sever ties with each other because they reminded each other of their childhood pain. Now they were going through the same questioning that she was, contacting each other to try to make sense of the strange behavior they were all experiencing. She suddenly recognized the blackness of her pain for what it was. She watched as one of her sisters, who had also turned to alcohol to quiet the pain, was transformed dramatically into a beautiful, calm, rational person. She decided at that point that she would become the same sort of person. So she sobered up too, swallowed her pride, and began to get help.

"All the time there were little miracles that I only now can recognize as coming from God," she explained. "God didn't open my eyes to the traumatic reasons for my pain until I was open to him because he knew I'd need his love to handle what I'd learn." Now Lori goes to several support groups on a continuing basis—Alcoholics Anonymous and Incest Survivors Anonymous to name two—and although she says she is still struggling to accept herself, Lori Yoder has become just as beautiful a person as her sister. She's still struggling, but more and more, with the help of God and others, she's aware of the source of her pain and is working hard to get past it to realize that God is in control and that he is always reaching out to her with goodness, love, and cleansing mercy.

Like Lori, if we can hear past our own private pain, we can lower the pain level in the ways that matter, in the ways that will help us cope. It's true, whatever loud form our personal pain takes.

The Power of Words

Words of truth have a power all their own to pierce such shrillness. You can see for yourself. Read the words of good news from Isaiah:

> *God is here.*
> *God is in control.*

Now, read those powerful words again slowly, silently. Listen. Block out all other thoughts, all other sounds. Let their meaning sink into your mind and stay there:

> *God is here.*
> *God is in control.*

See what I mean? Soothing and wonderful, the words, words of truth, can dull the pain and help us cope. God is here. God is in control. There is power in repeating those truthful words.

Be Still

How, you may ask, do we learn to listen past the pain?

At the turn of the century, there was a coal mine in England which coal miners continued to dig deeper and deeper into the crevices of the rock. It became a huge mine as they continued to pull from every new vein the precious coal which the cities of England needed to stay warm. This coal mine got larger and larger, deeper and deeper, and the fingerlike tunnels wound their way around into a great maze. The mine became so large that people became very fearful that one day someone would get lost inside. And that day came.

Four men were on their way back up to the entrance of the mine when they made a wrong turn. Only the kerosene lamps they carried kept the way lighted enough for them to continue to hunt for the opening, but hours passed without any sight of the light from above. The group of miners continued to walk around and around in the maze until their lights went out.

Total darkness, the kind in which you can close your eyes and open them and you can't tell the difference, the kind in which you can put your hand literally straight in front of your face and not see it, is a frightening thing. Total darkness conceals the distance between you and the person next to you, between you and the walls, between you and freedom.

I've known it once. While I was on a tour deep inside Carlsbad Caverns in New Mexico, the guides took us into a chamber and closed it off, just to give us the experience. I will never forget the eerie, frightening feeling.

These men found themselves in such a place, in total darkness, alone. One of the men suggested that they lie down on the ground and breathe as lightly as they could and see if they couldn't feel their way somehow out of that prison maze. So they tried it. The whole group lay there in the darkness, totally quiet, breathing as lightly as they possibly could. Finally one of them said, "I know which way to go! Everyone link hands!" They did, and for a few hundred feet, they moved. Then he stopped and sighed, "I don't feel it anymore."

"Feel what?" one of the men asked.

"The air," he said. "I felt a breeze."

So they all lay down again and breathed as softly as they could, patiently. After several minutes, one of the men whispered, "I feel it!" So they all linked hands again, and moved a few feet, and once more they lost it.

Finally, one of the men pulled out a match and lit it. All the men's eyes stared at the first light they'd seen in hours. As they remained perfectly still, they watched it flicker. One by one, the men realized the significance of the flame. It was flickering toward the source of oxygen—toward the way out. So burning match after match, the group followed the flicker of the flame until they saw the light from above themselves.

It's the same with us today. God is there. He is waiting. But God does not usually shout. His calling to us is often not more than a whisper. And when we cannot hear that whisper or see the flicker of his flame, then there is something we must do.

We have to be still. To know which path to take in life, to know which steps to retrace, to trudge on, we must be still, just as the miners were still, before we can know which way to turn. It is as the psalmist says. We should be still and know that he is God.

What does that mean in practical terms?

It means that we must *still* our anger, our depression, our disappointments. We must still the pain and anguish constantly streaming from our suffering, still them as best we can. We must clear our minds of the anxiety and the hurt and allow the good news that God is in control to come through. "Behold the Lord comes with a strong hand," Isaiah wrote. "Like a shepherd, he will feed his flock."

Isaiah tells us that we should be bearers of the good news. Such people have learned the secret of listening to God and the power of sharing such knowledge with others. That is the secret. We will hear it above the pain of our fragile spirits.

Be still.

Listen.

Don't allow pain to deafen you to the good news that God is in control.

"All flesh is grass
And all its loveliness is like the flower of the
    field. . . .
The grass withers, the flower fades,
But the word of our God stands forever."

Who has measured the waters in the hollow of
    his hand,
Measured heaven with a span . . .
Who has directed the Spirit of the Lord? . . .
Behold the nations are as a drop in a bucket,
And are counted as the small dust on the
    balance.

—Isaiah 40:6, 8; 12, 13, 15

Chapter 6

Whom Do You Trust?

What would you do if you heard a voice, not just any voice but The Voice?

You'd probably look this way and that and give your ear a whack; then you'd ask the people standing by, "Did you hear something? I thought I heard something."

Then just when you thought you'd imagined the whole thing, it happened again.

Cry out.

That's what the voice seemed to be saying.

You'd roll your eyes around slowly and get deathly quiet, waiting, waiting to hear it again. . . .

Isaiah told us he heard a voice. I can only imagine how he responded, but if there were a human bone in his body, he would certainly have responded in amazement. Maybe he even stuttered:

Cry out!

"C-c-c-ry out? Cry out what?"

And The Voice told him.

And he told us.

Isaiah had God's very words to share with us.

Getting Our Attention

If you were about to tell the true, accurate, without qualification, words of God himself, how would you get everybody's attention?

In our modern lingo, Isaiah would probably have said:

> Ladies and gentlemen, boys and girls, I must have your attention. What I am about to tell you is of vital importance. Listen to me; hear what I am about to tell you. Do I have your attention?
> A voice told me to call out.
> And I answered, "What shall I call out?"
> The message is this:
> Dear Friend:
>> Don't trust in yourselves.
>> Don't trust in the material things of this world.
>> Don't rest assured of anything—except one thing.
>> And that is the Lord.

Search for Something Solid

How often do we fight insecurity, pain, or loss? How often do we search for something to rely on. Every day we try to discover that single something or that certain someone that will be solid, never changing, concrete in slippery times.

In verses 13 and 15, Isaiah describes the only two options that he believes we have in that search:

- We can trust in ourselves, in this world and its material things—like the grass and the flowers of the field, or
- We can trust in God, the One who measured the waters in the hollow of his hand and the heavens with a span of his arm.

Whom will you trust?

The voice said, "Cry out!"
And he said, "What shall I cry?"
"All flesh is grass,
And all its loveliness is like the flower of the field.
The grass withers, the flower fades,
Because the breath of the Lord blows upon it.
Surely the people are grass.
The grass withers, the flower fades,
But the word of our God stands forever."
Who has measured the waters in the hollow of his
    hand,
Measured heaven with a span
And calculated the dust of the earth in a measure?
Weighed the mountains in scales
And the hills in a balance?
Who has directed the Spirit of the Lord?
Or as His counselor has taught Him?
With whom did He take counsel, and who
    instructed Him,
And taught Him in the path of justice?
Who taught Him knowledge,
And showed Him the way of understanding?
Behold the nations are as a drop in a bucket,
And are counted as the small dust on the balance.

—Isaiah 40:6–8; 12–15

Backyards, Front Yards, and Beautiful Roses

I take great pride in my lawn. I have a nice, thick, green natural carpet of a mixture of rye and bluegrass. I trudge out there three or four times a year and fertilize it meticulously. As soon as that thickness gets the slightest bit on the thin side, I hurry out there with the right amount of succulent nutrients.

It takes a lot of extra work, but when I look out the window and see that grass in all its velvety splendor and I step outside and smell its grassy fragrance, well, let me tell you, the time and effort are worthwhile.

Then there's the backyard. Our backyard was once like our front yard. But then we decided to add another member to the family—the kind with four legs and a tail. We spent weeks looking over the different pedigrees and came to the conclusion we needed a Doberman pinscher.

Within a matter of months, every screen on our house was gone, several pairs of my wife's shoes were chewed into small bits of leather, and the backyard—oh, the backyard. It looked like a patchwork quilt. Digging and running and burying his toys, our dog had made that backyard his own. Now I can mow the whole thing and get only half a bag of grass.

I look at the front yard, and then I look at the backyard, and I know exactly what Isaiah means when he says, "All flesh is grass." The grass withers. Boy, does it wither!

And the flower fades. . . .

Recently I bought thirty long-stemmed lavender roses. Why did I make such a gesture? My wife turned thirty. So I was extravagant, which is a good thing, by the way, for a husband to be occasionally. Like magic,

It is the natural human tendency to believe in God. It is abnormal not to.

those roses opened up slowly and wonderfully, a little the first day, a little more the next, and a little more the next. We were so awed by their beauty that every day we took pictures of them.

Then there was the fourth day. Half the petals were on the floor. By the next day, the other half dropped. The stems were dead, and the water was smelly. Within a few minutes on the fifth day, we had tossed it all out.

Again, I was reminded of Isaiah.

We are like grass, like flowers, he said, speaking the words of God. We are delicate, fragile, temporary.

On What Can We Rely?

Think of the things that give you a feeling of importance. If you are like most people, that is what you lean on, whether you are aware of it or not.

Is that one thing physical beauty? It will fade.

Is it money? We can lose it.

Youth? We know that won't last, yet our society has made it into a thing to be revered. When I am confronted with someone who is worrying about not being "young" anymore, I always respond by asking that person to try to recall life at age thirteen. I don't know about you, but I'm not sure I'd want to be that young again. Adolescence is not a happy time for the adolescent, no matter what tricks our memory may play.

All flesh is grass. Our bodies will wither and fade. We can delay the process by eating properly, by exercising, by making use of modern medicine's treatment advances, but we still must face the fact that our bodies will grow old just as the grass does, just as all living things do.

Nothing on this earth, then, is worthy of our all-out trust because nothing lasts forever, nothing is infallible. All created things change.

Which brings us to Isaiah's other option: the One who measures the waters in the hollow of his hand.

Who Measures the Water?

Who has measured the water in the hollow of his hand? Anybody you know? The big guy down the street? Nature is still the most powerful force on planet Earth, and we human beings continue to fight a losing battle with it.

Water covers 70 percent of the world's surface. In the Polynesian culture, the ocean is actually considered a demon force. In the Netherlands, the people have reclaimed most of their country's land from the ocean by building dikes and continuously pumping out the water. The moment they stop pumping, though, the patient, powerful water will reclaim the land.

Humans have always been in a constant struggle against nature, and no human has control of it. Obviously, no human can do what Isaiah suggested, either. No one but the Creator of nature could have the powers to measure the water. When I read Isaiah's question, I have a mental image of the outstretched hands of God encompassing not just the water but the entire universe. Who measures the heavens?

The sheer expanse of creation is awe inspiring. From the earth to the moon, it is 240 thousand miles. If you started walking up a stairway to heaven today, twenty-four hours a day at a pace of three miles an hour, it would take you eighty years to arrive. That's fast walking. Now, think about walking to Pluto or the Big Dipper. Think about going to Alpha Centauri. Those stars are so far away that many are no longer in existence, but their light, traveling at the speed of light, will twinkle for us for centuries to come.

But Isaiah didn't stop there. "Who weighed the dust?" he asked. Have you tried to weigh a speck of dust? To realize nature in its infinitesimal diversity is to realize God's magnitude and his attention to detail.

Are you aware of the small yet absolutely essential details needed for Earth to support life? The existence of life, in any form, depends on just the right environment.

- The Earth is tilted at a twenty-three-degree angle to the sun, just the right angle to receive the amount of heat needed for life.
- The Earth revolves at just the right speed. Otherwise our days and nights would be too long or short, and we would either freeze from exposure to frigid moon or burn from scorching sun.
- The Earth's orbit is just the right speed and distance from the sun. We are so fragile that if our temperatures totaled fifty degrees more or less in a year, we would die. So if the Earth's orbit was even the slightest bit slower or faster, it would be either pulled too close to the sun or thrown too far out in space, and it would be either frozen or molten.

Our creation is so precisely set that the smallest tilt of our planet's axis here or melting of the poles there, and neither of us would be here—that's how delicately balanced our fragile world is.

Who holds the waters in his hand? Who measures the heavens in a span and calculates the dust of the earth and weighs the mountains in a balance and the hills on a pair of scales?

The answer without question, without hesitation, is God, the Father. He was in the beginning, is now, and forevermore will be God.

Who Counseled the Spirit?

Then Isaiah asked, "Who has directed the Spirit of the Lord? With whom did he consult, and who gave him understanding and who taught him the paths of justice, knowledge, and understanding?"

To look at nature is to use words such as *enormous, delicate, immense, complex, awe inspiring*. When we look into ourselves, we use such words as *knowing, soul, instinct*. There is within the human soul an understanding that God exists. God reveals himself specifically to the heart and mind of each of us, to every person who lives on this planet. All of us know that there is some sort of Supreme Being. We know because we know.

Science can't explain such specific revelation. And usually the things scientists can't explain they will label "instinct."

In San Juan Capistrano where I live, the swallows are famous for doing something that comes naturally—by instinct. They return every March 19 to the mission here. It seems like magic, but it's quite natural. Something written in their genetic makeup tells them where to go and when. From Argentina, they fly en masse back to the very place they've been coming for centuries. What is the attraction? No one seems to know.

When the first mission, now the oldest building in California, was built here in 1777, the swallows took an instant liking to its structure and began to build nests, lots of them, in all its small alcoves around the crest of the fine building. Soon, they became a nuisance. The story goes that when others living and working at the mission wanted to take sticks and guns and drive them away, Father Serra took pity on the birds. "Where will they go?" he asked.

"Anywhere but here," an assistant is said to have remarked.

"No," said Father Serra, "their home will be here." Somehow the swallows have continued to come back each year, even after the church was almost devastated by a nineteenth-century earthquake, even after people began noticing the exact timing and faithful devotion of the swallows to the old mission. The swallows, for some reason, consider it home. Each year at the same time, they hear an internal call back to home.

Are we that much different? If we are as tuned to our inner spirit and call as the lowly swallows, don't we feel such a call, such a tug?

An inherent, natural driving force that originates from our divine creation and points us to our own place in creation is written in our makeup too. We are drawn as naturally as the birds of the air and the creatures of the wild are called by their inner voices. If we are in tune, we can still hear it.

Against Nature

If all of us have a natural tug, why are there people who seem indifferent to God? If not being drawn to

God is unnatural, what has happened to the person who isn't drawn to God? Something obviously is interfering with the call from within.

What would you think of a salmon that didn't swim up river? What would you think of a swallow that stayed in Argentina? What would you think of ducks that didn't fly south for the winter? Something unnatural would have to happen to take them off the natural path intended for them. When we don't follow that inner feeling that we were made for things bigger than ourselves by someone bigger than ourselves, then circumstances beyond our control have impeded that call. As we discussed in the last chapter, the pain assaulting our fragile spirits (be it physical, emotional, or spiritual) can drown out our natural pull toward God.

Beyond Instinct

There is another reason that we should be able to "tune in" instead of "turn off." Our specific revelation goes beyond instinct, which is just the first nudge. The rest is that God has specifically revealed himself to the human race through Christ. He has left no doubt in our intellectually superior minds. He can reside within us. And that is what makes us, of all the creatures God created, so special.

Who has directed the Spirit of the Lord? With whom did he consult, who taught him about knowledge and understanding and justice? In other words, what human in all his or her wisdom could direct God?

Inside us, we are hearing God's counsel, his direction, his presence—not the other way around. In a few short questions, Isaiah has pointed out the human folly of thinking we are smarter and wiser than the One who created us. We can handle life alone; we can live without God's presence; but if we try, we are living an unnatural life.

Drop in the Bucket

But how do the powerful countries of the world fit in? "Nations are a drop in the bucket" to God, Isaiah pointed out. In Isaiah's day, when one thought of power, one automatically thought of military power. A people's survival depended on it. The power of the nation of which you either are a citizen or a slave would have been constantly on the mind of the ordinary shepherd, farmer, carpenter, or weaver of Isaiah's day. If you were talking power in a group of such folk, surely their eyes would grow big with the mention of, perhaps, Babylon or Persia or even the Philistines.

So it's natural for Isaiah to add the nations of the known world to his comparison sheet. Israel, even then, was obsessed with being a nation and all that goes with a sense of pride and ownership and "Don't tread on me" independence. They couldn't help being awed by the great powers of their world who had the power to do quite a bit of treading.

But what does Isaiah say? These nations, with all their soldiers and strength, are trivial—nothing—a drop in a bucket—less than dust on a scale—compared to the one who spread his arms and created the universe. God can use nations or throw them aside whenever he chooses.

Isaiah actually proved his point in the very next chapter. Isaiah told of how God would choose a king named Cyrus of Persia to lead his Persian army in a victorious battle over Babylon after Nebuchadrezzar's death—for one reason. He would have Cyrus, whether Cyrus knew it or not, allow the exiled Israelites to return home under his rule. And that is exactly what happened.

So whom would you depend on? A nation? Yourself? The grass of this earth? Or would you depend on the Being who uses nations to his own ends, who created the heavens from nothing, who has placed his imprint deep inside you? Isaiah said that the answer is obvious, the alternative absurd.

Depending on the Wrong Things

But that doesn't keep us from choosing the alternative, does it?

Not too long ago, I was driving down the freeway with a close friend of mine when he told me something that shocked me. Suddenly, he told me that there had been a time in his life where he never started a day without a snort of cocaine. The drug gave him a temporary high feeling of self-esteem, a feeling that he could conquer the world. The feeling was so wonderful that he was using cocaine the way we would a cup of coffee. Every morning he took his vial full of the drug, opened it, tapped a little bit out, and sniffed it.

The abuse didn't stop there, though. Soon, whenever he felt a little insecure, he took his little upper, and instantly he was able to handle the world again. That's the

way he lived for a very long time until one day he realized that he could not go on without serious complica-
tions, and finally he took steps to stop. He knew it
would be hard to give up the drug he had relied on for
so long, but he didn't know how hard until he decided
to give it up. He told me that every morning was a struggle for a very long time.

I hear many stories such as my friend's, but I'm
always surprised. Soon after that drive on the freeway,
a woman shared with me at church how she had so
abused cocaine that the drug ate away at the inside lin-
ing of her nasal passages. She had to have reconstruc-
tive surgery on her nose.

Whatever the dependency is, be it alcohol, illegal or
legal drugs, food, or even obsessive behavior such as
bulimia, it affects the people you know—maybe even
you yourself. These people are good people who recognize they need help, something to rely on, but they
choose the wrong things.

Robert Schuller Ministries touches so many different
types of people from so many different backgrounds
that we often see how easily the search for something
to rely on can lead down the wrong path. Recently
we've realized we should be doing something to reach
out to people whose pain leads them to such self-
destructive behavior. So Robert Schuller Ministries has
begun the New Hope Treatment Center, which mixes
psychology, religion, and possibility thinking to help
people who have begun having trouble with compulsive and debilitating phobias and behaviors such as depression, anxiety, drug and alcohol abuse, destructive
sexual behaviors, overeating, and anorexia. The center

is a place that can touch all areas of a hurting person's life and give him or her the strength to find the reliable path once again.

Overwhelming pain can strike any of us. We are so fragile. We are so dependent as we boast of our independence. No one, though, goes it totally alone. We all find things to lean on, and too often they are not healthy for us. All the deadly crutches mentioned above make up the modern response to our modern pressure-cooker world.

Wavering in the Wind

Let me ask you a question:

If you were to choose the most serious thing everyone is guilty of what would it be? Cheating? Stealing? Lying?

We all may be guilty of one of these, but the real sin that makes these seem insignificant is lack of trust. One of its major aspects is that it gets in the way of our relationship with God; it makes us less than what we were meant to be. A lack of trust in the fact that God is capable of meeting our needs is surely our greatest failure. When we begin to doubt that God can give us the strength to handle anything and everything life throws our way, we waver in the wind, we worry, and we put our faith in undependable, unpredictable people and things. Our confidence comes and goes. We undermine our own potential, and we become like the grass.

But once we've seen God's presence—the light—in the difficulty in our lives, we know there is another way. And such experiences make it easier to trust him.

That, I know, is "easier said than done," as the saying goes. However God himself has shown us a way to build trust in him.

A Way to Build Trust in God

Richard Lobs, minister of St. Mark's Episcopal Church in Geneva, Illinois, explains this Old Testament concept as well as anyone I know. He tells how the people in Joshua's day also had trouble relying on God. After the Israelites wandered in the wilderness for forty years, God finally allowed Joshua to lead them into the Promised Land. God stopped the flow of the Jordan River so that the Israelites could cross over, just as he had parted the Red Sea forty years before. Even after that miracle, though, the people were still afraid. Maybe they had become blasé about miracles after being fed manna from heaven and led by pillars of smoke and fire for a generation.

But the real trouble was that they were worried about the change they were about to make. In only a few days, they would be expected to feed, house, and clothe themselves. They would also be expected to stay in one place after so many years of being nomadic. Many were fearful of such a change. They couldn't make themselves trust that God would help them, as he'd always done. Their memory was as short as ours is.

So, at a place called Gilgal, Joshua asked the people to do two things. First, he told them to take twelve boulders, one for each tribe of Israel, and place them in the middle of the Jordan River where it was all dried up. When the waters came back, they would not be able to see these stones, but they would remember they had put them there. And he told the people that when they remembered those stones, they should remember the twelve boulders as a pillar of testimony to the power and to the hand of God on their behalf, drying rivers for them, parting seas, leading them to their Promised Land.

But Joshua didn't stop there. He told them next to take twelve more stones, one for each tribe of Israel, and set them at Gilgal. These stones would be left for the future as a visual pillar of testimony to remind their children of God's mighty power and ever-present control.

Joshua was showing the Israelites that remembering is the key to trust. If they could remember what God had done for them in the past, they would find it easy to trust God for the present and the future.

That's true for us, too, of course. When we feel like wavering, we must make our own pile of stones, invisible ones, like the ones in the Jordan River. Some people keep a journal, in which they record the ways God has—and is— helping them. This journal becomes their "pile of stones," reminding them that the great things God did for them yesterday, he will also do for them tomorrow.

Truer words were never spoken. What we choose to trust is our choice, and sometime, somehow, we will trust something.

Isaiah told us the unvarnished truth: A voice cried. Listen. That is important. Do I have your attention?

This will change your life. Put your trust in God. He will never fail you, and you can build a meaningful, confident, secure life on him.

Have you not understood from the foundations
  of the earth?
It is He who sits above the circle of the earth.
And its inhabitants are like grasshoppers,
Who stretches out the heavens like a curtain,
And spreads them out like a tent to dwell in.

                                    —Isaiah 40:21–22

Chapter 7

Small Among Giants

M

y father met a very interesting woman at one of his Bible studies at the Crystal Cathedral. She was tall enough to tower over my father. Considering my dad is six feet, two inches tall, it was quite a surprise. My father listened attentively as the woman made jokes about her height until she mentioned that she was the president of the Tall Women of California Association. My father, caught off guard, responded, "You're kidding. There are other women as tall as you are?" *Whoops!* he thought.

But she answered matter-of-factly: "Oh yes, there are many. In fact, I'm one of the short ones."

There are, of course, many people physically bigger than you and me. Remember when you were a kid? The school bully was no doubt bigger than you and the other kids on the playground.

I also remember feeling small back then in another way. I was one of those students who would sit in the very back corner of the classroom and pray, "Dear Lord, don't let the teacher call on me. Please . . . oh, please." I was enormously intimidated. I felt like an intellectual midget in my extremely smart class.

Small or Tall?

When you feel small and insecure, it's horrible, and the feeling doesn't go away with age. Ideally, we grow out of such feelings of insecurity, but we don't ever to-

141

tally grow out of them, do we? Even as adults, we can feel small as grasshoppers, and the feeling wreaks havoc with our fragile spirits—and drastically weakens our potential.

Because of my father, I've been in the company of many VIP types—people with political, religious, financial, and communications power—many of whom are on the *Hour of Power* board. I became a member of the board of *Hour of Power* when I was twenty-eight. I sat in the same room, meeting after meeting, with people who have done great and mighty things in our country and world and who feel strongly about trying to do great and mighty things for the Lord. Picture yourself in the same room, meeting after meeting, with such people as Norman Vincent Peale, the much-loved minister and author who's also president of Fleming Revell Publishing Company; W. Clement Stone, the enormously successful businessman and investor, who is chairman of his Combined International Corporation; Buert Ser Vaas, chairman of the board of Curtis Publishing Company; Richard De Vos, president of Amway Corporation; William Dearden, retired chairman of the board of Hershey Foods Corporation; Helen Exum, vice-president of *Chattanooga News-Free Press;* and the list could go on. For quite a long time, I felt I had no right to be there.

Over the years, I've been in enough such situations that I've been forced to analyze the feeling and learn how to feel "great" in the midst of great people such as these. How do we feel great in a room full of giants, whatever or whoever those giants may be? How do we feel confident enough to fight against gigantic, tower-

---

*Prayer is
taking one step
toward God.*

ing problems? Isaiah knew the secret of true self-esteem.

Grasshoppers and Goliaths

At the time of Isaiah's writing, the story of David and Goliath was still very fresh in the minds of his readers. That story was to them what our Boston Tea Party and Washington Crossing the Delaware stories are to us, part of their heritage.

By all accounts, David was not a big man. And Goliath—well, I'm sure he grew in the minds of the people over the years—but we know he terrified the soldiers who had to battle him, so he must not have been any shrinking violet.

Think of the Israelite readers of Isaiah's words, then, and of the time they were living in, full of fear of outside giant nations that could come as Goliath did and trample them underfoot. These Israelites were filled with fear of their own giants.

Ever since David's day, they had fought off giant nations—Persians, Syrians, Babylonians, Egyptians, Philistines, Assyrians. All of these warring nations wanted to trample the little Promised Land underfoot and carry the booty away.

In their weaker moments, Israel's kings made alliances with one or another of these marauders, hoping to get protection of a sort, like paying protection money to a bully to keep yourself safe. Sometimes they stopped listening to the babble of their advisors and their enemies and listened to their prophets, as when God killed that horde of Assyrians overnight to save

King Hezekiah and Jerusalem. But those times were few and far between. Even when they were at their strongest, during the time of Isaiah, the kings still looked in the wrong place for their courage and security—to themselves.

And so Isaiah scolded them: "Have you not heard? Has it not been told you from the very beginning? From the foundation of the earth, it is God who sits above the circle of the earth and its inhabitants are like grasshoppers."

Grasshoppers? That's quite an image—the human race as small and insignificant and fleeting as grasshoppers. I believe, though, that Isaiah used that comparison not to make us feel small but to make us aware of what the human race as a whole looks like when compared to the almighty God.

Haven't I Told You Before?

I detect a certain tone in this part of Isaiah's words. Do you hear what I hear? I hear the tone of a father scolding his children.

I am a father myself. Right now, one of my children is at an age when he chooses to be deaf. In one ear and out the other go my words. "Bobby," I say, "clean your room."

"Yes, Daddy."

Ten minutes later, he is still sitting in front of the television set.

"Bobby, what did I tell you?"

"Oh, yeah," he says, and off to his room he runs.

A few minutes later, I stop by his room, and it is still a

mess, and in the middle of the mess, Bobby is playing. "Bobby—" I scold.

Sometimes, as all children do, he does things for which his father must punish him. I have a strict process for punishing any of my children. I scold, hold, and then mold.

After I punish Bobby, he usually cries, big tears streaming down his cheeks. "Bobby," I say, "you know I love you."

"I love you too, Daddy," he says.

Then we hug each other, and I say, "Bobby, it's okay," and I pat him on the back. "When I talk, you listen. Do what I tell you to do so I won't have to scold you next time," I explain, in hopes of molding him to do better. I want to leave him with a new image of what I want him to be.

Isaiah, then, sounds like a good parent. He knew the Israelites were not listening and so he began with a reprimand.

He said, "You know you shouldn't feel intimidated. You know you are just as good as everybody else. You already know these things, so why do you feel the way you do? Your God is a God so big and so powerful that he sits in the heavens looking down on the grasshopper residents of this world. That is your God. He is the One who reduces rulers to nothing, who makes the judges of the earth meaningless. He is the One who can kill 185,000 Assyrians overnight to answer a prayer. He is the One who will manipulate other nations to allow his people to go home. Tiny Israel, you've got almighty Yahweh—God. You should feel strong and secure and good about yourself!"

Translate Isaiah's message into the here and now. It works doesn't it? Who are these people, these things, that are making you feel small? Is it the woman at work who always looks as if she popped off the cover of *Vogue?* Is it the smart young assistant at work on his way up? Is it the twenty-four-hour day you need to get through without a drink or a pill? Is it the "Super-Mom" of your child's best friend? Is it the bills that your paycheck never quite covers? Is it the Joneses you feel pressured to keep up with? Maybe it's the boss who doesn't seem to know you exist? Or is it that relationship that has taken a wrong turn?

Your God is bigger than any of them. With a puff of his cheeks he can blow them away. So why don't you feel great? Why don't you feel terrific? Why don't you feel full of dignity and self-esteem?

True Dignity

When we compare ourselves to the world, I think most humans have a tendency to measure themselves and their dignity by their place in society and their earthly power. But here the prophet Isaiah shares with us the true source of dignity in a personal relationship with God. God doesn't care about nations, as Isaiah told us earlier in this chapter. "The nations are as a drop in a bucket," he said, "and are counted as the small dust in the balance." The nations are here today and gone tomorrow in God's scheme of time.

As I mentioned in chapter 6, God can manipulate other nations, the very ones that Israel saw as giants, toward his ends. Isaiah told Israel that God would actually use King Cyrus of Persia to allow the scattered Israelite slaves to go home. And he did. Nations are but puppets to God.

Look throughout history and see how nations have come and gone. Babylon is a good example. When was the last time you met a Babylonian? They were the majestic rulers when Isaiah 40 was written. King Nebuchadrezzar was the outstanding king of his age. During his reign, the Babylonians overran Assyria, which had already conquered Israel's Northern Kingdom. Then for fourteen years they attacked and ultimately conquered the Southern Kingdom where Jerusalem stood. Then, whenever they felt like it, the Babylonians came and took Israelites captive, and the people of God were very frightened of this seemingly all-powerful nation.

But where is Babylon today? It has vanished.

Where are the Israelites? They are in their homeland, a powerful nation, determined to survive, quite successful today at keeping neighboring nations at bay.

What Does Count?

What counts then? I believe Isaiah was suggesting that it is the individual. God, your God, the God who is always with you, who loves you and guides you and made you his own, is more powerful than nature, than human wisdom, than any nation that has ever existed. And he is actually there for you, he knows your name, among all of his creation. He knows where you are and is reaching to touch your soul with his strength.

As Isaiah said, "He calls them all by name. In the greatness of His might, and the strength of His power, not one is missing." Not one!

Not too long ago, a movie called *Rainman* was playing across the country. It was special, not because it starred Dustin Hoffman, who is a wonderful actor, or Tom Cruise, who has been blessed with good looks and talent. It was special because it was about the relationship between a young know-it-all and his older brother, who happened to be autistic.

An autistic person is not mentally retarded, although he seems strange to the casual observer. Instead, autistic people are those whose brains are getting mixed signals, so to speak, and they live in their own private worlds, hardly ever touched by others or able to touch others in normal, human relationships.

In *Rainman* Dustin Hoffman played an autistic man superbly, so achingly well that it sometimes hurt to watch. Yet during the course of the movie, his life, a life that seemed wasted and worth little on first glance, changed his selfish brother's life entirely. The younger brother was made more human, more caring and loving, just by being exposed to this seemingly wasted, worthless life.

Even more touching was the newspaper account I read later about how an autistic boy saw the movie with his family and then somehow was able to write Dustin Hoffman a letter. The article told how the autistic boy thanked Hoffman for portraying autistic people in a good light because his performance helped the autistic boy see that he was worthwhile in his autism.

The worth of the individual has nothing to do with what the world thinks. The worth of an individual has everything to do with what the individual's Creator thinks. Our Creator thinks so highly of us that he sent his son to suffer and die for us. "He gives power to the

Have you not understood from the foundations
    of the earth?
It is He who sits above the circle of the earth.
And its inhabitants are like grasshoppers,
Who stretches out the heavens like a curtain,
And spreads them out like a tent to dwell in.
Lift up your eyes on high,
And see who has created these things . . .
He calls them all by name,
By the greatness of His might
And the strength of His power;
Not one is missing.
He gives power to the weak,
And to those who have no might He increases
    strength.

—Isaiah 40:21–22, 26, 29

weak," wrote Isaiah, "and to those who have no might he increases strength."

God felt that way in Old Testament days about one nation and its people. In fact, he thought so highly of Israel that he chose it to be his. He picked one man, Abraham, to found this special nation, and as it grew, God was there. He slew armies for his people; he parted seas for them and guided them and fed them in the wilderness. He picked rulers to lead them; he promised them a land and helped them attain it. He kept them safe from harm even when they ignored him. But just as a loving parent would do, he also warned them when they were wrong, then warned them again, and when they would not change their ways, he punished them.

But that's not the end of the story. Because what did he do after all of that?

He always, always forgave them. Over and over and over, he forgave them.

He only did that for one nation—Israel.

"I AM YOUR GOD," he told them. That should have been enough for any Israelite to know he or she was special.

I can't help but think about the prophet Hosea's story. In his Old Testament book, Hosea unceasingly searched for Gomer, his wayward prostitute wife, finding her and taking her back only to have her run away again and again. Yet he always forgave her and found her once more. It is quite a metaphor for God's persistent love for his chosen people.

And, just as we discussed in chapter 6, the most wonderful part of the story is that today, because of Christ, when we give God control of our lives, we become one of that special group called his people, *his chosen peo-*

ple. Psalm 139 does a superb job of expressing how special we are to him. "O LORD, You have searched me and known me. . . . Such knowledge is too wonderful for me. . . . How precious also are Your thoughts to me, O God! . . . When I awake I am still with You."[1]

"Don't you understand?" wrote Isaiah. "He calls you by name!"

Being Held

So Isaiah scolds and then holds, just as I hold my son after I scold him.

In a comforting tone, Isaiah seems to be saying, "Listen, little one. Who stretches out the heavens like a curtain? Like a tent for you to dwell in? Who is it that cares for you? Who is it that listens to your prayers? Who is it that gives you strength when you are tired and confused?"

Maybe you can remember a time when you felt insignificant and intimidated and suddenly a peace swept over you, bringing you to a sense of the grand scheme of things. Perhaps you were in danger, and you felt a sense of peace pass over you. Perhaps the moment was just a quiet one in which you felt a sudden surge of unexplainable peace. If so, it was a time when you realized suddenly that God is with you. You are one of God's special people, chosen, directed by God. He is yours, and you are his.

If you've ever felt that way, even for a moment, you have known the power God promises to his people. "He gives power to the weak," says Isaiah, "and to those who have no might he increases strength."

Vic Andrews is a close friend of mine. One day, he

told me an experience he and his wife June had that still gives me chills. In 1961 he and June decided to take a trip around the world. Vic was a grower for the Sunkist line, the huge company that sells oranges all over the world, so he arranged for his wife, himself, and another couple to travel on one of Sunkist's freight-moving ships.

The accommodations and services exceeded their expectations. They were the only passengers on board. Each night they dined with the captain. They began the trip thinking it would be the trip of a lifetime. They turned out to be right, but not in the way they had expected. Within hours, the seas turned bad, with seventy-foot waves crashing over the ship. Vic described it as surfing in a freighter. The experience was not pleasant, and it lasted for six weeks. The waves were crashing against the ship so hard that no one could walk on the deck for fear of being washed over.

Finally, on February 6, 1961, a date the Andrews will never forget, the ship approached the coast of Japan. The sea finally subsided enough for them to relax and even walk the deck. That evening, the captain did not dine with them. He stayed on the bridge to guide the ship toward the harbor. Instead, the first mate dined with them. In the middle of their pleasant meal, three blasts of a loud horn pierced the air. The first mate stiffened, then jumped to his feet, saying, "I am needed on the bridge immediately." Before he could reach the door, the most incredible wrenching sound Vic had ever heard drowned out everything else. Imagine the sound of two ships colliding, of metal wrenching and tearing as twenty thousand tons hit twenty thousand tons. That was the sound.

Everything went dark. It was pitch black. There was no sound, no power, no lights—nothing. That's when June reached out and grabbed the hands around her at the table and said, "Be calm. Be still. God will take care of us."

Finally, they all stood up and began feeling their way back to their cabins for their life jackets. When they got them, Vic and June and their friends had to part company. The Andrews were assigned to a lifeboat on the port side, and their friends' boat was on the starboard side. They did not know if they would ever see each other again.

When Vic and June finally made their way to the port side, they saw a shocking sight. The crew was struggling with the lifeboat. Each lifeboat was built of solid steel, weighed over a ton, and was equipped to carry sixty-five people. The ship was a modern freighter, so everything worked off hydraulics and electricity, even the lifeboats, but the collision was so severe that there was not even enough power left to lower the lifeboats. The men were desperately trying to pick up a corner of the boat, hoping somehow to push it into the water.

It was painfully obvious that the ship was not going to stay afloat. When the two ships hit, they hit bow to bow, and the result was a peeling back of the entire side of the ship, like the paring off an apple or a lid being peeled off a sardine can. If the other ship had cut their ship in two, their chances would have been better. They might have stayed afloat by sealing off the less-damaged side. That is not what happened, though, so in minutes the ship was listing, and the captain made the call to abandon ship.

When the crew heard the captain's words, they quit

struggling with the lifeboat and stood deathly still. June, at that moment, let go of Vic's hand, and began walking toward the front of the ship, holding onto the rail as the ship dipped at a twenty-five-degree angle. She called back, "I'm going to pray." June, who has studied opera, picked a special way to pray. In the stillness of the next few moments, all that the crew and Vic heard was June's beautiful voice singing the Lord's Prayer, "Our Father, who art in heaven. Hallowed be thy name. Thy kingdom come, thy will be done, on earth as it is in heaven. . . ."

Nothing but stars shone that evening. There was still no light, no power, and no sound, save the sound of June's voice lifting to the night sky over the sounds of the cracking and moaning of the huge freighter as it started its way to the ocean's floor. There on that sinking ship, June, in glorious fashion, was reaching out to her God as one of his children desperately in need of his power.

Then the captain made the expected second call: "abandon ship." On the top of the boat were small life rafts, which would detach and drift in the water. The goal was to find one of those rafts and wait for help. Some of the first ones overboard could slide down the hull because the ship was already on its side. The last ones could walk down the hull. Vic and June, though, were behind even the last ones because June was having trouble getting over the railing, and before she could manage it, the ship surged and flipped completely on its side. Suddenly the pair were hanging onto the rail with their feet dangling at least seventy-five feet above the water. The only thing between them and that seven-story drop was an open hatch. Vic let go and fell to the door. Then he looked up at June and said, "June, you've got to let go. I'll try to catch you."

June said, "You're going to *catch me?* That's a good one. Here I go." Fortunately, Vic broke her fall, but he could not control it, so they both tumbled into the water below.

It was February and the water was icy cold six miles out of the Yokohama harbor. They knew that because of the severity and swiftness of the accident, the captain had not had time to radio for help, but they tried not to think of it. All he'd been able to do was send up three flares. Three single shafts of fiery light were their only hope.

But Vic and June had more to worry about than rescue. June did not know how to swim, they had fallen below the freight area, and in the dark they had to dodge falling crates and cables and pulleys. They had to swim away from the mess. So with June hanging onto his life jacket, Vic, who grew up swimming on a California beach, began to swim out of the way of the danger. Unfortunately that headed them in the opposite direction from the rest of the group. Soon they were away from the ship, but they were also alone in the dark, in the freezing cold water, watching the stern of the ship turn upright and go down. It disappeared before their eyes.

Vic began to swim again, even though he could see nothing, and he bobbed into something. Quickly he realized it was a crewman, face down. Vic lifted his head, and the man gasped, "Life raft that way," and then fell unconscious. Vic grabbed the man by his hair, keeping his face out of the water so he wouldn't drown, and began to swim once again, June still holding onto his lifejacket. In a few seconds, they could hear the sound of people in the raft. In another few seconds, they were holding onto the raft. The raft was already so full that it was a foot too low in the water. So all Vic and June could do was hold on and pray. "Be still, be calm," June had said when it all began. "God will take care of us."

When a faint glimmer of light appeared on the horizon, no one spoke for minutes. The water was so cold that many were beginning to hallucinate because hypothermia was setting in, and they did not trust what they saw. Then everyone began to scream and yell at once. The glimmer of light was coming from a small boat being rowed by two Japanese men, sent out to see if there were any survivors by a nearby ship that had seen the flares. Finally the ordeal was over. They were saved. Six people died in the accident, but Vic and June recovered from their icy swim, and their friends, though badly cut on the jagged edges of their side of the ship, also survived.

Vic and June knew the God who "gives power to the weak." Whether we ever find ourselves suddenly in deadly peril as the Andrews did or not, all God's children experience being held by God at one time or another as we move closer and closer personally to the Almighty. A close walk with God, the kind of close relationship in which the almighty God calls us by name, ensures that each of us can call upon him to give strength to our own fragile spirits.

The Armor of God's People

What does calling upon him entail? The answer is natural. The act of calling upon him is prayer. Praying is taking our step toward God and his control. It's such an easy step for such an oustanding privilege. To be brought into God's presence with a few words and to be filled with his strength—it's a gift we take so for granted. Yet it is the way he can fill us with his strength for any situation. Prayer, then, is like the fragile spirit's sword and shield. Put on the whole armor of God, Paul tells us in Ephesians, "praying always with all prayer and supplications in the Spirit, being watchful to this end with all perseverance and supplication."[2]

There is such power in words lifted to him. And as we make calling upon him a steady part of our lives— then we will experience his strength in the most natural way, no matter what giant looms over us.

Feeling Like a Giant

When my daughter Christina was eighteen months old, she fell and hit her head. We began to worry about her and decided to take her to the doctor. The doctor assured us there was probably nothing wrong but to alleviate our fears he was going to have a few skull X-rays taken. So we went into the X-ray room, and I put Christina on the table. She cried a bit, but I comforted her, and soon we were looking at the pictures of her skull. The X-rays showed that she had a skull fracture.

We went home to wait for the doctor to call. When he called, he said he couldn't tell the severity of the fracture from the X-rays, so he wanted us to take Christina to see a neurosurgeon.

The next day we met with the neurosurgeon who scheduled a CAT scan. Since Donna was pregnant at the time and couldn't be exposed to the radiation from the test, she couldn't go with us into the CAT-scan room. I had to handle the situation myself.

The room was filled with a huge, donut-shaped piece of equipment. It was six feet high and at least three feet wide. We were told by the attendants that Christina was to place her head inside the machine and lie perfectly still for four minutes to get a clear picture. If she moved a fraction of an inch, the technicians would have to start over.

I thought to myself, *How in the world will we ever get her to lie still that long?* One of the attendants suggested giving Christina a sedative. I said, "You seem to know my daughter very well." Even though I realized the sedative made sense, I was hesitant. So I had Christina lie down and place her head on the black foam cushions inside the machine. Then I suggested to the attendant that we try it without the sedative. *Fat chance,* I thought to myself, but I wanted to try. She immediately began to squirm. I handed her bottle to her, and right away she calmed down. For a moment, I thought it might work. It did until they gave me a lead apron to put on and one to put on Christina.

That's when Christina decided that things were looking a bit scary for her tastes, and she began to cry. Wiggling with her arms outstretched, she began crying the words that melt any daddy's heart: "Help me Daddy! Help me!"

Behind a glass partition, a nurse talking through a speaker told me to hold her still. So I realized that there was only one thing that might work. I turned to Christina and said, "Let's pray, Christina."

She immediately folded her hands around her bottle

and lay perfectly still. I prayed, "Dear God, thank you for . . ." and I began a list of every relative, every friend, every part of Christina's body I could think of. Finally, I exhausted the list of things to pray for so I said, Amen.

"Amen," Christina said.

The nurse bellowed, "Keep it up a little longer! That's perfect." So we began to pray again. Finally, the four minutes were up, and we said another amen and relaxed. Soon we were told that the test showed she would be fine.

Christina, a tiny little girl, was dwarfed by a huge machine, and prayer calmed her.

That speaks volumes to me. A fatherly touch, a prayer, and a stillness in the presence of a bad situation calmed Christina through her small crisis. She felt peaceful in the presence of giants. It's the same with all of us.

The God who made us—who sometimes scolds us and always holds us, who is bigger than any problem we have—wants us to feel big and strong as giants through him. He wants us to realize that we are his people. Special. Made by his own hands. With God's power and love surrounding us, all of our problems can truly be reduced to a manageable size.

Why do you say, O Jacob,
And speak, O Israel:
"My way is hidden from the LORD,
And my just claim is passed over by my God"?
Have you not known?
Have you not heard?
The everlasting God, the LORD,
The Creator of the ends of the earth,
Neither faints nor is weary.
There is no searching of His understanding.

—Isaiah 40:27, 28

Chapter 8

Reason with Yourself

At age twenty-one, Anthony T. Rossi sailed into New York Harbor. It was 1921, and although he had only a little over a dollar in his pocket, he soon got a job, saved, and bought his first grocery store.

He grew up in Italy, a devoted Catholic boy who had never thought too much about Christ—or Christianity, for that matter. But he was a man of unflagging cheer, and fueled by his ambition and dreams, his business thrived. The way he threw himself into any enterprise, with all his heart, showed in all his dealings. He was so curious, always full of big ideas, lots of big ideas.

One big idea was to have the first self-serve market in New York. He decided he'd market as many fresh fruits and vegetables as he could. This wasn't an easy task in the 1930s. But he was determined with his whole heart, so he got up before daybreak to go to the open markets, select the best produce there, then bring it back to his store. He loved fresh fruits in cold New York.

One day, a regular customer of Tony's, a young woman he'd noticed every time she came in, asked if she could leave her groceries with him while she went to the butcher shop around the corner. "Certainly," he said. And while she was away, he placed some very large, very heavy cans in the bottom of her grocery sacks.

"I didn't realize these were so heavy," she said, when she returned.

"Don't worry," smiled Tony, "I'll have someone deliver them to your apartment later."

"That would be wonderful," she said.

Later, Tony delivered those groceries—with his whole heart—and before too long, he had married Florence. "Florence," he said, "New York is too cold. I've got a better idea. Let's go to Florida. I want to farm." Without further ado, he sold his market and began to make plans.

The fact that he didn't know anything about farming couldn't stop a Tony Rossi big idea. He went to the library to read about it. There he noticed a book that someone had forgotten to shelve. It was called *The Life of Christ*.

Realizing, suddenly, that he really didn't know anything about Christ except that he was a baby in the Madonna's arms and that he died on the cross, Tony opened the book and began to read. As he turned page after page, he forgot all about farming for the moment. Hours passed. He was totally engrossed. He put the book down late that afternoon and went out to find a Bible.

By the time he'd gotten to the fourth gospel, he stopped cold at John 3:16. The message was so clear, sincere, consistent. And with his usual fervor—his whole heart—he took a giant leap in his personal faith. As he trucked off to plant tomatoes on fifty acres in Florida, he did not know that he was only taking the first steps in what would turn out to be an amazing process inspired by spiritual and professional fervor. Now God was going to be a part of his big ideas and dreams. As he grew in faith, so would his big ideas.

Balance:
the correct concept
for living.

Deep Spiritual Life

Is it possible for us to develop as full human beings without a deep spiritual life?

That question is brought up on a regular basis in our society. Most people seem to agree that a person needs to be spiritual, but it's a "not now, but later" kind of attitude. Many people think, "Sure, I think being spiritual is important, but not right now. I'll think about it later, though." They're like the teenager who says, "Hey, I believe in God. I just want to have my fun first. I'll get concerned about religion when I'm old."

Isn't it strange that we don't think of fun and God in the same context?

But another irony of life is that a deep spiritual walk with Christ makes life fun. They are one and the same. If you wish to have a life more fulfilled, more rewarding, more relaxed and enjoyable, then you should take steps to deepen your spiritual side.

Believe it or not, medical science is beginning to find evidence of that fact. In a recent *Psychology Today* article, one of the first researchers to describe Type A behavior was quoted as saying, "Spiritual need may be the underlying crisis among Type A people prone to heart attacks." A University of California study of business people under extreme stress—telephone managers during "Ma Bell's" breakup and oil executives during deregulation—found that there was a special trait in the hardy ones who thrived while others suffered heart attacks: they were deeply spiritual.

The article also discussed a man named Herbert Benson, author of *The Relaxation Response,* who has been on *The Hour of Power*. He has been writing about prayer's role in producing sharp reductions in heart beat and blood pressure for several years. He is now involved in new experiments pointing to a correlation between greater spirituality and health improvement.[1]

All this research has been going on for the last several years, and we will see more about it in the future as even science realizes that human beings are more than just blood and bones. Medicine is beginning to tell us that we are better off when we realize that we are spiritual beings.

In short, a deep spiritual way of life is the best of all lives.

What then does it mean to have a deeper spiritual life?

The Deeper, Balanced Spiritual Life

Isaiah 11:2 speaks of the spirit: "The Spirit of wisdom and understanding, the Spirit of counsel and might, the Spirit of knowledge and of the fear of the LORD."

These six gifts of the Spirit are worthy spiritual principles for us. When we make them a part of our balanced spiritual life, our spirits grow deeper. But we must first know another "Spirit of . . ." before we can understand these principles. First, we must know the Spirit of the Lord. The Spirit of the Lord is the balancing beam upon which other spiritual principles in our life find their balance. Then we juggle the rest until we can walk calmly and confidently on that beam, grasping every principle in a full and deep way.

Balance has always been the correct concept for living. We've been told for years how important a balanced diet is for health, for instance. Now we have a formula for a balanced spiritual life.

Notice the way the quotation is phrased. The sentence itself is balanced. Wisdom is balanced with understanding—a person must have wise insight to truly understand anything. Then counsel is balanced with power. If we have one without the other, abuse of either is easy. And last, knowledge must be weighed with fear—or respect—of the Lord. How can one truly respect the Lord, or "fear" him in the positive sense that a person is meant to, without correct knowledge of him?

To understand how important these balances are, let's look at another portion of Isaiah.

Wisdom and Understanding, Counsel and Power

Earlier in Isaiah's ministry during the reign of King Ahaz, Judea—the Southern Kingdom—was confronted with Israel, the Northern Kingdom, along with neighboring Syria.[2] Their leaders told Ahaz that they were very worried Assyria was going to invade their lands. So they told Ahaz he must join with them to invade Assyria first; if he did not join with them, then they would attack him, too.

King Ahaz was intimidated by Assyria, as well he should have been. At that moment in history Assyria was the most powerful nation in their part of the world. If you recall, in chapter 2 we discussed how Assyria finally conquered the Northern Kingdom. Ahaz was certain that joining in an attack on Assyria with Israel and Syria would be totally disastrous, and he would not do it. Instead, he decided to contact Assyria for protection from his two neighbors.

In walked Isaiah at this point. I am sure Isaiah was not one of King Ahaz's favorite people. From all accounts of his ways, King Ahaz was probably one of the forerunners of the slide into moral decay that Isaiah preached against during his first years as a prophet. Ahaz was infatuated with pagan rituals and introduced many of them into Judah while he was king. He made images to Baal, actually practiced infant sacrifice, and even established a heathen altar from one of his foreign trips in the temple of the Lord alongside the one that held the Mosaic Law. To top that off, he opened and closed the temple on his whim and even broke some of the sacred vessels on purpose. Isaiah, I'm sure, had already filled his ear with words of the Lord many times.

This time, though, the message was more urgent and personal than usual. "Don't align with Assyria," Isaiah told Ahaz. "God has said that your neighbors will not succeed in their plan, so quit worrying."

Ahaz was not convinced. He decided to go ahead and send a proposal to Assyria with some expensive gifts.

So, in essence, God said, "Listen, Ahaz, if you want me to protect you, then you better learn to believe what I say."

Still Ahaz turned a deaf ear.

So God responded, "Ask me for a sign, Ahaz. Go ahead. Let me prove to you that I can crush your enemies as I've said. Ask anything you like, anything."

What did Ahaz say? "I will not ask, nor will I test the Lord."[3] And he went ahead and made his pact with Assyria, sending it along with the expensive gifts to its king. Within a few short months, Assyria had already taken advantage of Ahaz. Its king was forcing him to pay tribute, and Ahaz had to watch in terror as Assyria wreaked havoc throughout the region.

Ahaz did not understand about balances. He was teetering one way, then tottering the other. He could not grasp the correct counsel for where true power lay. So ultimately he made all the wrong choices.

Ask for a Sign

God comes to each one of us, and he says, "Ask the Lord, your God, for a sign. Whether you're in the deepest despair or the deepest sorrow, whether you're in the depths of frustration or struggle, test me. Put me to the test."

He said it to Ahaz. Why would he not say it to us?

Every time I've challenged people to put God to the test in this way, someone comes up to me and says, "But isn't it wrong to test God?" And then they quote me the New Testament words of Jesus: "Thou shalt not tempt the Lord thy God."

Is it wrong?

Is It Wrong to Ask?

Shortly after he was baptized, Jesus went into the wilderness to fast. There Satan appeared and tempted him, and as he was being tempted, Jesus quoted that passage of Scripture that so many people quote to me. The Scripture is an Old Testament one, found in Deuteronomy, and actually says, "You shall not tempt the LORD your God as you tempted Him in Massah."[4]

Massah was a stop on the wilderness wanderings of the Israelites during the Exodus. For years, manna fell from heaven for them to eat every night, and every day and every night they had a pillar of fire or smoke to lead them.

But even with all those needs met, they questioned. There was a period of time in which they found no water. They probably needed an enormous amount. So one day, many of them began to grumble and challenge Moses' leadership. "Is the Lord among us or not?" they asked.

Things were quite tense when Moses asked God for help. "What am I going to do, Lord?" The people's asking such a question angered God and tempted him to do away with all of them. But instead, God told Moses to lead the people to Mount Horeb where he would meet Moses at the rock. There Moses would strike it with his staff, and water would come gushing forth. That is exactly what happened. Moses named the place Massah which means "tempting Jehovah to slay us."

What is the point, then? We are not to test God to see if he is "among us," to see if he exists. Why? Because that knowledge is integral to our knowing the Spirit of the Lord, the balance beam of our spirituality. God is there. We must believe that without continued questioning. So to test God in that sense is the "shalt not" we should obey.

But we *can* test him to *know the truth*. In other

words, we can venture ahead in situations in which we need his guidance, as a test to find out what direction we should be going in our lives. There is a passage in Malachi in which God actually tells the people to test him: "Bring all the tithes to the storehouse . . . and prove Me, . . . if I will not . . . pour out for you such blessing that there will not be room enough to receive it," he essentially states in 3:10. "Let me prove it," is the way one translation puts it.

In Isaiah 40 God also asks, "Why do you say, 'My way is hidden from the Lord? And my just claim is passed over by my God?'" It's just not so, Isaiah wrote. "Have you not seen? Have you not heard? The everlasting God neither faints nor is weary."

Gideon's Fleece

When many people think of testing God, they think of Gideon "putting out the fleece." Actually that is exactly what he did. He needed guidance from the Lord on how to save his people from the threat of a warring tribe. He needed to know whether or not to go into battle. So he decided he would test God's direction for him. Since his own and many others' lives were on the line, he had to make the test clear. So he said, "Lord, I tell you what. I've got this fleece, this lambskin. I'll leave it outside my tent tonight, and if you want me to go into battle, please make the fleece wet with all the ground around it dry in the morning. If it is, I'll go." So he went to sleep and in the morning, the fleece was dripping wet.

But Gideon began to worry. "You know, maybe it

would have been wet without my prayer. So to make absolutely sure that God wants me to go into battle, I'll try again tonight. Lord, if you want me to go into battle, let's do this in reverse. Instead of wetting the fleece, make the fleece dry and the ground all around it wet. Okay?"

The next morning, he woke up, slid in the mud all the way to the fleece, and picked it up. It was bone dry. The answer was clear.

Jesus said it this way: "Ask and it will be given to you. Seek and you'll find. Knock and the door will be opened. For everyone who asks, receives, and everyone who seeks finds. And to everyone who knocks, the door will be opened."

God and Oranges

Anthony Rossi broke all the rules with his Florida tomato patch. He was so excited about his first season that he prayed about everything, since God was so much a part of his thinking and dreaming now. "Father," he prayed, "if I make five thousand dollars net profit on these tomatoes, I will be satisfied."

Things began to look so good that Tony began thinking he would do much, much better than that, until time to pick the tomatoes. He could not find enough experienced pickers. They had all been hired earlier by the established growers nearby. Unfortunately, most of his tomatoes rotted before he could get them to market.

Florence tallied their books, though, and found they had still done all right. "We made five thousand dollars anyway."

Tony laughed. God had heard him. Then he laughed

again and said, "I should have asked for ten thousand."
But the reality of a God who was there and was in communication with him, who would guide his plans and
dreams, left Tony almost breathless.

What followed were years of different businesses—
cafeterias, restaurants, a fruit basket business—every
one guided by Tony's dreams and prayers. He was beginning to learn that as long as he was in tune with
God, he could begin to act on his ideas, and God would
show him quickly if it was the way he wanted Tony to
go.

One of his big ideas was to ship fresh orange juice to
the fancy hotels in New York. The hotels were paying
women to come in every morning and squeeze fresh
oranges by hand, because fresh orange juice was such a
delicacy in the early 1950s before refrigeration was per-
fected. Through "impossible" ideas such as leasing
freight trains on which to squeeze and move orange
juice at the same time, he founded Tropicana Orange
Juice Company. And idea after idea, things came together. One by one, he hired men who thought like him
and who believed like him until soon Tropicana was being called the "Christian orange juice company." Tony,
though, never rested on his monetary success. He was
always taking all he made and trying new and uncertain
ideas.

He sank five million dollars, almost all Tropicana
had, into a new state-of-the-art warehouse designed
to keep his orange juice fresh tasting until it was
shipped—"fresh-chilled" it would be called. During
the celebration party, though, the building burst into
flames. The great idea burned to the ground.

In the morning, one of his assistants looked at him

and said, "I'm sorry, Tony," believing the fire might have dealt Tropicana a fatal stroke.

Instead of being miserable, Tony was smiling. "I have an idea," he said. From experience, he knew God would be faithful to answer him even during a crisis if he stepped out in faith with his ideas—and this new one was a big one. It would require bankers and other creditors and all the company's investments to back him in trying another thing that had never been done. As always, it was a gamble. He was going to buy a ship and overhaul it to take his fresh-chilled juice to New York the way an oil tanker would take oil. He threw everything into the project.

And the *S.S. Tropicana* was born. Many of the engineering problems that such an idea raised were said to be "impossible," too. But somehow every idea worked. And as he watched the *S.S. Tropicana* slide into New York Harbor for the first time, he knew that God had been faithful once again. He had tested God for the direction he should go, and God had answered him with a resounding "yes."

Anthony Rossi, whose success story would appear in *Forbes* and *Fortune* and who would receive an honorary degree from Tampa University, began with little formal education and a fledgling, practical relationship with God. He ultimately sold Tropicana to Beatrice Foods and with the money set up the Aurora Foundation, which now funds Christian missions and educational institutions, among which are Bradenton Missionary Village in Florida, a planned housing development for retired missionaries, and Bible Alliance, which produces Christian products for the blind. He is a modern Gideon who knew that having a deep spiritual walk was the only way to live, and he walked it moment by moment, risking with big ideas, knowing God was faithful to tell him when he erred and bless him when he was right.

Testing God in Tony Rossi's fashion is part of growing deeper in your spiritual life. In asking for God's direction and not being afraid to fail and try again, you can deepen your understanding, your wisdom, and your experience with God's counsel and God's power. Wisdom and understanding, counsel and power, a balancing act, but a balance which is part of a deep spiritual walk.

Knowledge and Respect

The last set of spiritual gifts—knowledge of and respect for God—comes with a balanced walk, too. How do we receive knowledge? God told the Israelites, as Moses wrote in Deuteronomy: "Therefore you shall lay up these words of mine [the Bible] in your heart and in your soul . . . that your days and the days of your children may be multiplied" (Deuteronomy 11:18–21). It is fascinating to me, however, that modern scientists and doctors frequently discover the accuracy of biblical truth.

The Healthy and Hearty

In *The Trusting Heart: Great News about Type A Behavior,* Redford Williams, a behavior medicine specialist and heart disease expert, gives twelve steps to better, longer living.[5] I have no idea whether Dr. Williams is a Christian, but many of these steps can actually be found in God's plan for our lives in the Bible. Notice the points. The Scripture passages are my additions:

1) *Monitor your cynical thoughts.*
"Whatever things are true . . . noble . . . just . . . pure . . . meditate on these things."[6]

2) *Confession is good for the soul.*
"Confess your trespasses to one another, and pray for one another."[7]

3) *Stop those thoughts.*
"For out of the heart proceed evil thoughts. . . ."[8]

4) *Reason with yourself.*
"All things work together for good to those who love God."[9]

5) *Put yourself in the other person's shoes.*
"Whatever you want men to do to you, do also to them."[10]

6) *Learn to laugh at yourself.*
"To everything there is a season . . . a time to laugh . . ."[11]

7) *Learn to relax.*
"Come to Me, all you who labor and are heavy laden, and I will give you rest."[12]

8) *Practice trust.*
"I will trust and not be afraid."[13]

9) *Learn to listen.*
"Be swift to hear, slow to speak. . . ."[14]

10) *Learn to be assertive.*
"Ask, and it will be given you, seek and you will find; knock, and it will be opened to you."[15]

11) *Pretend today is your last.*
"Do not worry about tomorrow, for tomorrow will worry about its own things."[16]

12) *Practice forgiving.*

"For if you forgive men their trespasses, your heavenly Father will also forgive you."[17]

Isn't it interesting that medical science is rediscovering the age-old biblical truths? It's an unusual testimony to the power of biblical knowledge for our lives. In fact, three of these steps—monitoring our thoughts, practicing trust, and practicing forgiveness—are found in the exercises to strengthening our fragile spirits: speaking comfort, learning forgiveness, and trusting God. I find it fascinating that even though the sermons that form the basis for this book were preached millenniums before Williams' book was published, his points can be found in God's words to Israel, truth that is applicable to healthy living today as well as yesterday.

Obviously, then, reading and memorizing God's words will help us know what is good for our minds, bodies, and spirits. Isaiah tells us to have the spirit of knowledge. With it, we can know more and more deeply the God worthy of our respect and devotion.

What happens when you develop a deep spiritual life? You start living healthier lives, better lives, more joyful, exciting, strengthened lives.

Our way isn't hidden from the Lord. As you make these spiritual powers your own, you'll see God working in your life. You'll feel him in your decisions and your future. Test the God who neither faints nor is weary. He will answer.

But those who wait on the LORD
Shall renew their strength;
They shall mount up with wings like eagles.
They shall run and not be weary,
They shall walk and not faint.

—Isaiah 40:31

Chapter 9

Waiting on the Lord

A mother is in anguish over her son's jail sentence for drugs. There is nothing she can do but wait, and the waiting seems hopeless. What can she do now for her child?

Last summer, a young man, his company's golden boy, had the world by the tail as he moved across the country to set up a whole new branch for the firm. Today, he is a victim of cutbacks, without a job, far from home and friends. All he can do is wait.

An athlete on his way to a world class competition breaks an Achilles tendon and finds himself flat on his back in a cast. He will never compete again. In fact he is told he will be lucky to walk without a limp, much less run. A lifetime of devotion to one calling, his whole future, is gone. Where is the hope?

Today, in growing numbers, people are living on the streets. We call them the homeless. For various reasons, they have ended up without a place to call home, without a friend who will take them in. Life has done them in, and they've given up. They scrounge through our trash to survive. If they find enough money for a phone call, they don't call to find work or shelter, they buy a cup of coffee or a donut. These are people without hope.

Most of us will never know the depth of physical

need of the homeless. Most of us, though, have known the emotional and spiritual agony of life on hold, of being forced to wait, feeling hopeless and weak and utterly directionless. The sense of desolation can be devastating. Easily we can be convinced that hope is gone.

No Respect

Hopelessness is no respecter of persons. Yet hopelessness is a lie. All of us have hope, if we will only listen. That is Isaiah's final message to us in chapter 40.

The prophet has taken us full circle. Opening with assurance that God will redeem and restore Israel, he closes with an inspirational charge. All that has been said before will come to nothing unless we do one very important thing:

We must learn to wait on the Lord.

Those Who Wait

For the average Israelite to whom this message was aimed, being told to wait and still hold on to hope was a mighty big order. But if you can do it, Isaiah said, there's a promise involved. You will be given the patience, the strength, and the power to make it and great will be your reward.

Those who wait on the Lord, he is saying, will renew their strength. To those in chains in Babylon, to those in fear in Palestine, he says: Wait. Be patient. Hold on.

Hold on.

Hold on!

Positive waiting is active not passive.

Who among us hasn't felt captive to circumstances beyond our control? Facing challenges and problems and frustrations, we can hear these same words: *Wait. Be patient. Hold on.*

And if we do, here is the promise:

We will mount up with wings as eagles, we will run and not be weary, we will walk and not faint.

God's Timing

Waiting was a way of life for the Israelites, yet sometimes the waiting surely seemed unbearable.

Their nation in chaos, scattered so far it would never be the same, their way of life all but gone, their past lying in heaps of junk—and now they were to wait and have hope?

Their thoughts and energy were probably set on survival above all else. How could such people still have hope? Many probably didn't make it. They probably took up the lifestyle of the country they were in and settled for peace at any price. It would be understandable. How could such a people understand that God's timing is the same size as God's greatness?

Then and now, God's timing can be excruciating and often unfathomable. It takes a lot of faith to trust so deeply in God's love and mercy that we can wait patiently during those in-between times in our lives. The idea of mounting up on eagles' wings was no doubt an impossible dream for the ancient Hebrews, just as it seems to us in our own waiting patterns. That is the promise Isaiah offered the people of God, though, and Isaiah meant every word.

Instamatic World

Those who wait on the Lord learn to know God's timing rather than the frenetic pace of our instamatic world. We have instant potatoes, instant oatmeal, fast food, one-hour photo processing. We have microwaves that melt butter in a handful of seconds. We have cameras that do everything but click the shutter for us. We can hop on a plane and be in Paris in a little over three hours. Soon, as one airlines boasts, we will be able to get to Tokyo in an hour. That sounds unbelievable, doesn't it? It's only a matter of time, though, before we will take such speed for granted, as we do with all our other conveniences.

Ours is definitely an instant gratification lifestyle. Waiting is delayed gratification, and that has all but lost its meaning in our modern have-it-done-yesterday society. Our great-grandparents couldn't have kept up. The "old-fashioned ways" have taken on nostalgic overtones, but they are in no danger of a comeback.

I admit that some of our instant things are better than the old-fashioned ones, but not all of them. Anybody who has had mashed potatoes done the old-fashioned way would never choose instant potatoes instead. Yet instant potatoes still sell, so many of us don't mind sacrificing taste for time saved.

Living in a society like ours makes waiting on anything, even the Lord, almost unbearable, almost impossible. It certainly makes it harder than it has ever been in the history of our race. But old-fashioned can at times be better. The trick is in the waiting.

What do I mean? Isaiah's promise states that if we

wait on the Lord, we will run and not be weary. If we cannot run, we will walk and not faint, and whenever possible, we will mount up on wings as eagles and soar right through whatever we are facing—when we wait on the Lord.

Waiting Is Not Sitting

The waiting that Isaiah is talking about, though, is not the kind that keeps us twiddling our thumbs.

There is a joke I love about Billy Graham, Oral Roberts, and my father. The joke begins with all three dying on the same day and finding themselves in front of St. Peter at the pearly gates. But there is a problem. "Hey, I'm sorry," St. Peter explains. "We have a full house today. We weren't expecting any of you so soon, much less all three on the same day. But I know you must all be tired after all you've done on earth, so I tell you what. We have lots of rooms below if you don't mind a little heat and a lack of a few amenities. Why don't you stay down there a short while, and when your mansions are ready, we'll bring you right up. Just enjoy your rest as much as you can. You've earned it."

So Billy and Robert and Oral go to hell. Days go by. Finally, one day, Satan himself knocks on the doors of heaven. "Listen," he says to St. Peter, "you've got to get those guys out of there."

"Why?" says St. Peter. "They're just waiting."

"Waiting, ha!" Satan spits. "That's a laugh. Oral is healing everybody, Billy is trying to convert everybody, and that Robert Schuller guy is raising money to air condition the place!"

These men have obviously gained a reputation for waiting actively. When Isaiah says wait, he doesn't mean sit.

Power Through Doing

Art Burcher is a wonderfully successful businessman, on top of his world. All was going right for him until two months ago. One morning, he woke up with pains in his legs, pains so bad that he couldn't walk. He went to the hospital and soon learned that he had acquired a rare spinal virus that causes paralysis. Only rarely do people recuperate from this virus on which little research has been done. With the help of his friends, though, he has rejuvenated himself enough to walk. His habits have changed drastically. He has to watch every step he takes and never takes any movement for granted.

While visiting him one day, I asked how he felt.

"Well, Robert, my legs feel like they are really cold, so cold it hurts, and the pain is chronic. The doctors say there's nothing to do but wait," he told me.

"But how do you deal with that waiting?" I asked.

He smiled, and answered, "Let me tell you something. A little while ago, several nuns came into my office and asked me to chair a building project that will cost millions of dollars. I didn't really want to do it, but I said yes. That night, I thought about what I had said, and I could not figure out why I had agreed to something I didn't really want to do, especially considering my health. Then I realized that I had said yes because it was a good way to wait on the Lord."

When we wait on the Lord, we aren't meant to sit. There is power in "doing." We are not to be so inward that we do nothing. It's critical for us to move. If we do not, we are saying, "Okay, Lord, it's up to you, and I'll just wait," and that will only slow the process down. Why? It's easier to steer a moving car than a parked car. God deals with lives that are working and moving.

It is possible to wait and to act. How? Almost all of us can pat our heads and rub our tummies at the same time. While we are waiting on the Lord through our problems, we can be doing, and the results of acting can be extraordinary. We at our church have seen this dynamic in action. When our church helped the people in the ravaged Mexican town of La Carbonera, we helped ourselves. As we reached out to help someone else, our own burden seemed lighter, and soon our burden was lifted.

How can you act? The possibilities are endless, big and small.

A Small Need

One Manhattan resident has found a small way. Like most of us, Michael Greenberg always had sympathy for the homeless he saw, especially during frigid weather. But Michael Greenberg is very unlike us in one way. He did not let the overwhelming size of the social problem keep him from doing something. He decided that as he waited for more powerful people to remedy the problem in a big way, he could act in a small way.

For the last ten years, he has privately gone out and bought wool gloves. He looks for sales. He may buy a pair for a dollar, he may buy a pair for two, but he buys and buys all year long. Then from Thanksgiving to Christmas, he passes out these gloves in the neediest part of New York City, the Bowery. In that area, lines of poverty are drawn differently. To be cold is to be poor, to be warm is to be rich.

Of course, the numbers are still overwhelming. He usually gives out four to five hundred pairs a year, but he could have passed out a thousand pairs a day, the need was so great. The first time he took gloves to the Bowery, Michael Greenberg realized that fact, and he was once again overwhelmed. He had already decided to act, though, and he was going to help. So he made a decision. On his trips, he seeks out the individual who is too down and out even to look at him as he passes. He touches the person on the shoulder, seeking to make contact; then he offers a pair of gloves. He says, "This is for you, no strings attached. It doesn't cost anything. They are yours."

Even at Home

You don't have to look far to find a need you can act upon. Ours is a fragile world. Why don't we take steps to minister to God's nature around us, for instance? Look at what we've already done to damage the ecology and how easy it would be for an unthinking government simply to blow it all up. Look at our family structure, endangered by all sorts of outside forces threatening its happiness and its very existence. The balance for both the family and the world is delicate. While we wait, we can act.

What can we do? When it comes to our world, we can be like Michael Greenberg. We can fill small needs while we are waiting for the government to do what it must to save the ecology. We can plant a tree, we can recycle our newspapers, we can use fewer styrofoam and plastic products, and we can conserve energy. As we do, we will strengthen our world, our spaceship earth, and surprisingly, our spirits, too.

As for our families, we can strive to make our family relationships stronger, kinder, and more complete. Strife seems to begin at home, and the pain we can feel from those we most love is sometimes unendurable. But we can act while we wait, by going the extra mile with our family members, by listening more, by trying to understand another point of view, but most of all by accepting and loving as God would. And again, we might be surprised how doing so might strengthen our fragile spirits in ways we'd never have guessed possible.

Waiting Is Growing

Waiting, then, is an active thing, not passive. At the beginning of the book, we discussed how comfort was active, not passive. Waiting gets its power in the same way. Much of the effort to make our fragile spirits strong comes from true effort—active effort to act in positive ways. Believe it or not, we can be growing spiritually as we wait. We can do what we can, instead of focusing on what we cannot do.

Why is action important? Action strengthens muscles—be they physical or spiritual. We are building our muscles so that when the time is right, we'll be able to wake up one morning and say, "I can do today what I couldn't yesterday."

Growing is the progression we know to be true in both our physical and spiritual lives. As babies we first learn to roll over; then we learn to stand; then we learn to crawl. Then we learn to walk, and then run. And, as Isaiah promised, quite often we soar.

Soar with the Eagles

Mount up with wings like. . . . "Soaring" is the way another translation puts Isaiah's famous image.

What is soaring? It's different from flying. It's moving through the air without flapping wings, without effort. Eagles are amazing birds. If you've ever seen one soar, you won't quickly forget it. Eagles lock their wings once they are spread out to their ten-foot span. Once locked, those wings allow the eagle to glide effortlessly on the currents for hours. Because of those special wings, the eagle keeps aloft not on its own power but on the currents. That's soaring.

It is this image of soaring that inspired *The Hour of Power* to begin our Eagles Club, our support base for all our ministries. Through the help that "eagles" all over the country give us, we are able to continue helping fellow Christians know the joy of walking, running, and soaring as God helps them. This Scripture is quoted on everything we give away to members of the Eagles Club, just to remind them of the wonderful promise of Isaiah's words.

The promise of soaring is real in this terrific Scripture. Isaiah said we can have this power, this effortless gliding on the currents of our lives. When we face struggles, the power of God will soar through our souls and give us the ability to mount up with the kind of wings he gave the eagles. The effort will not be ours.

How is it done? The secret is in the waiting. Learning to wait on the Lord can lead us to the means within ourselves to mount up—as strengthened spirits in this fragile world. And God gives us a support system to help us endure our difficulties as we wait.

Support System Built by God

What do you think a support system built by God would look like? Sturdy beams holding up a mountaintop cathedral? Or a bunch of fellow strugglers helping each other? The latter doesn't sound too strong, but there is true power in the concept—power to hold you and lift you and help you regain your strength when your spirit is its most fragile.

Actually, the concept has more to do with mountains than strong beams. All through the Bible, mountains are mentioned. In an earlier chapter we talked about what Isaiah meant when he wrote that we should get ourselves up onto a high mountain. The mountain image speaks to us today, too. We think of problems as mountains to climb. We also think of mountaintops as places of exultation and sometimes meditation. "Mountaintop experience" seems to be a term for spiritual moments. Isaiah himself said that we should go up to the mountain and worship God.[1]

Christ's support system is on the mountain. Those fellow strugglers should be fellow church members because our churches are God's support system for us.

How is this true? Just as a doctor will help us if we are

ill, our churches are there to care for us, too. To keep ourselves physically well, most of us have regular checkups. To keep ourselves spiritually well, we need to use our God-given support system called the church regularly, too. Jesus Christ established the institution called the church to comfort, to care, to support, to strengthen the spirits of his people. Our spirits are like batteries that need to be recharged. Perhaps, then, it's not a coincidence that when we decided to build Rancho Capistrano Church we picked one of the highest points on our land.

Meeting with other believers in worship of God renews our lives so that we can carry on for another week. Without worship, life is just that much more difficult; our spirits are just that much more fragile. Alone, we may find it more difficult to say yes to God and no to things that take his place. Alone, waiting on the Lord is often impossible. The church helps us stay on the mountain.

The Church Not There

The natural urge to have such a support system can still be seen in Jerusalem, and the mountain image is still alive and well there. One of the most important mountains in the Holy Land is Mount Moriah. Why? Because there the Holy of Holies and the original Hebrew Temple stood. It is also no doubt the mountaintop that Isaiah alluded to in his open letter to his countrymen.

Today, though, that mountain has changed dramatically. It no longer holds the Holy of Holies. In fact, it is no longer a place where the Jewish people come to worship and hasn't been since the destruction of Jerusalem after Christ died. Instead, it is an Islamic temple called the Dome of the Rock, the most holy Islamic shrine outside of Mecca. It's a phenomenal sight, golden in the Middle Eastern sun.

On the side of that mountain, where the temple once stood, Jews are allowed. On any given day, scores of Jews visit what remains of an old wall, which is all that remains of the Hebrew temple of biblical days. It is now known as the Wailing Wall. If you were there, you would see these Jews come and go with their Torahs and phylactery boxes wrapped on their wrists and foreheads. You might even hear them play different instruments as part of their worship. It is the closest they can come to being on the mountaintop temple of their ancestors.

If you've seen films about the Holy Land, you've inevitably seen the Wailing Wall, and you've inevitably seen another part of the worship. The wall has been called the "Lord's mailbox" because as these people pray they actually write a little prayer on a slip of paper, wad it up, and stick it into the cracks of the wall, jamming it down as far as they possibly can, in an attempt to get their message a little closer to God, no doubt, by getting it further into the temple.

Christianity doesn't have a Wailing Wall. With the birth of Jesus Christ, we see that the Lord's house is his church—not just walls and floors and pews. The church's strength does not lie in the brick and stone of its walls but in its people, in the support and guidance that arises from meeting together and helping each other. Isaiah has said, "Come, and let us go up to the mountain of the LORD, to the House of the God of Jacob; He will teach us His ways, and we shall walk in His paths."[2]

So we go to the Lord Jesus Christ's church. We go to our own "mountain." In support from other strugglers and in giving support to other strugglers, we find strength for our fragile spirits to walk, to wait, to run, and even perhaps to soar.

One of the most poignant and timely stories about the wonderful difference God's support system can make for our fragile spirits is a story in a recent issue of the magazine, *Marriage Partnership*. It is the story of Mark and Shireen Perry and their church, Covenant Church in San Francisco.

Mark and Shireen met in San Francisco at a conference on Christianity and the arts. They began dating, and after several months, Shireen decided to tell him about her deepest hurt. "It's been eight years ago this month that I became engaged," she began, and then she told him of their breakup because of her fiancé's homosexuality.

Mark listened intently, then said, "That's interesting, Shireen. Because eight years ago I also was engaged. But I broke it off to pursue the gay lifestyle, too." Then he went on to tell her that after several years, he began to question his lifestyle, and he gave it up for a time of soul searching that eventually led him to a very real, personal relationship with Christ.

Shireen wasn't shocked. They talked for hours, and afterward, they continued to date. Soon they fell in love. They were going to get married. Everything seemed wonderful.

Then only months after the wedding, Mark noticed a spot on his arm that did not go away. He went in for a routine examination and found out that he had AIDS. For several months, Shireen and Mark tried every kind of medical treatment, then slowly realized they had to tell their friends and family. What Mark worried most about, though, was the reaction of their church friends. Since his conversion, they had come to mean the world to him, and he was worried they would now reject him.

So Mark and Shireen went to see their minister, Mike Ryan. Mike agreed to set aside an entire Sunday evening service for Mark to talk to the congregation.

On that Sunday night, as Mark told of his former life, his conversion, and now about learning he had AIDS, the congregation listened, and they responded. One by one, they came down and crowded around him, and in a sign of love over fear, they all began touching Mark, holding hands, and surrounding him with prayer.

And then the nightmare of his disease began. Through the depression, through the anger, through the pain and weakness, through the growing acceptance, Mark and Shireen were supported. Their church friends supported Shireen as she coped with the ups and downs of Mark's physical and mental condition. And their love for Mark never slowed down. In the months that followed, the people of the Covenant Church began a twenty-four-hour prayer vigil for Mark and Shireen, asking for specifics to pray for, keeping in constant contact with them.

Mark and Shireen contacted a hospice organization to come to their house to care for Mark so that he would not have to be in the hospital. And when it became clear that they did not have enough staff to stay with Mark all day long while Shireen worked, the church organized volunteers to be there.

Other church members didn't wait to find out how they could help. From picking up prescriptions at the drugstore for them, to reading a book onto a tape and leaving it for Mark, to cleaning their house, to financial assistance, to prayers, Bible reading, and just plain getting together to laugh and have fun—the congregation was there for Mark and Shireen until the day Mark died. One member named Lucy Ogden, who happens to be a nurse, actually moved into their guest room and tended to Mark during the night those last few weeks so that Shireen could rest.

Then, after Mark died, the church was there to support Shireen. Even now, on tough days, she feels free to call her church friends and ask if she can just come over and read a book with them, just to be in the same room with friends who care.

Mark and Shireen's story is one of a church committed to active, enduring love and support in *any* situation, the kind of church support system that God intended for his children.

When tough times come, when our goal is to walk and not faint, a lonely struggle is much harder. God gave us the church to support us in those times.

God's Runners

Look around your church. Look at the diversity of people. One of the most interesting things about God's church is that each one of us has our own built-in pace.

There are days that each of us run, other days when we must wait, others when we walk. And although we all yearn to soar as much as we can, everyday living usually finds us with our feet firmly planted on the ground. So whether we run one day, soar the next, walk another, and then wait for weeks on end, we all have a normal stride, whatever speed it may be. We need to recognize our God-given speed and feel comfortable with it, or we will never be able to wait on the Lord.

Isn't it interesting how different people have been gifted by God with different abilities for use in God's kingdom? Some are meant to run. We know many of those runners by name: Billy Graham with his ability for evangelism and communication; Oral Roberts with his gift for healing; my father with his gift for spiritual motivation and renewal. These are men of God who know how to run, and when they are called on to wait on the Lord, they have learned how not to get weary.

God's Walkers

But if you'll notice, most of us in God's church are walkers. And we are just as cherished and nourished by God.

In 1982 an athlete named Bob Weiland spoke to our church of his dream of walking across America. For me to walk across America would be a major undertaking. How much more so for Bob Weiland, who lost his legs in Vietnam. But Bob Weiland walks anyway, and he walked across our country. The walk took several years, but he did it.

To walk across America with no legs, he had to extend his arms in front of him, swing his torso through, then bring his arms in front of him again. On his hands he wore gloves and on the fingers of his gloves he had big pads hardened into hooflike leather.

Why did he want to put himself through such an ordeal? He decided to walk across America because he had a message of hope to share. It's possible to succeed, he told people. He always shared his faith during his walk as he talked to papers, to major publications, including *People* and *Us,* and to church congregations along the way.

Think for a moment about that accomplishment. Bob didn't soar or run. He walked on his hands. Inch by highway inch, his is a story of walking and not fainting. His waiting on the Lord gave him that strength.

People like Bob make a difference. They run and they walk and they learn how to keep going, even when they feel like fainting. Don't think that sort of attitude doesn't reach far and wide among the people they touch. They are being all God wants them to be.

Tortoise Power

Sometimes all we can do in this tough world is to continue to walk without fainting. Yet there is a very real power in such tenacity. The tortoise can beat the hare, as the old story goes. There can be miracles even in that kind of waiting.

I was watching a baseball game recently. The team I was rooting for, the St. Louis Cardinals, was behind four runs in the eighth inning. The announcer, for some reason, suddenly was talking about the story of the tortoise and the hare. He told the fans how the hare dashed out in front in the race and seeing how far he was ahead, began to take it easy, figuring the race was his. "But remember that tortoise?" the announcer said. "It just kept plugging along."

Then he compared the hare and the tortoise to the two baseball teams. "The Cardinals have been known to be like the tortoise, tenacious and 'never-say-die,'" he pointed out. "With a hit there, and a hit here, and another hit there, who knows? The hares—they better watch out."

That's exactly what happened. The Cardinals had a hit here and a hit there, nothing spectacular. But the runs began to come in, and before anyone knew what was happening, it was the end of the game, and the Cardinals had pulled ahead just enough to win.

Maybe you're a tortoise instead of a hare. Tortoises were created to be tortoises. Often we forget the wonderful value of the tenacious tortoise, the strength in persistent, rock-steady walking.

This is the kind of walking Isaiah explained. Some of us are built to run. But most of us are built to walk, and if we wait on the Lord, if we never give up, we will definitely grow—and at the right moments we will know the feeling of soaring, mounting on wings of eagles. It happens when we persevere.

Isaiah's Rousing Ending

Isaiah has reminded us who God is; he has reminded us who we are in relationship with God and how wondrous a position that is. He has reminded us that God offers us who wait on him the courage and the strength to place our faith in our God.

Like a cheerleader, he ends with a rousing pep talk: Listen all of you who are God's people, listen to me! Wait on the Lord.

Walk, run, soar through all your troubles—you can do it if you learn the secret of waiting. You can "run and not be weary." You can "walk and not faint."

Remember this: Your spirit may seem fragile today. But I tell you now, there is strength waiting for you. Believe it. It's true. The keys are simple, and they are now yours.

Notes

Chapter 1   Strength for the Fragile Spirit
1. Luke 4:17.
2. Matthew 13:14–15.

Chapter 2   Speak Tenderly
1. Isaiah 2, 11–12, 24–27, 59–66.
2. Amos 4:1–3.
3. Isaiah 1:18.
4. Isaiah 2:3.
5. *Psychology Today,* Dec. 1988.

Chapter 3   Forgiving and Forgetting
1. Isaiah 1:11–13.
2. Matthew 18:21–22.
3. Isaiah 1:18.
4. Lewis Smedes, *Forgive and Forget* (San Francisco: Harper & Row, 1984), 29.

Chapter 4   Searching for Peace
1. Romans 7:15.
2. Fred LeFever, "A Changed Life," *Guideposts,* July 1988, 35.
3. Isaiah 40:5; Luke 3:6.

Chapter 5   Can You Hear the News?
1. 2 Kings 18–19.

Chapter 7   Small Among Giants
1. Psalm 139:1, 6, 17–18.
2. Ephesians 6:10-18.

Chapter 8   Reason with Yourself

1. T. George Harris, "Heart and Soul," *Psychology Today*, Jan./ Feb. 1989, 50–51.

2. Isaiah 7.

3. Isaiah 7:12.

4. Deuteronomy 6:16.

5. Redford Williams, *The Trusting Heart* (New York: Times Books), 148.

6. Philippians 4:8.

7. James 5:16.

8. Matthew 15:19.

9. Romans 8:28.

10. Matthew 7:12.

11. Ecclesiastes 3:1, 4.

12. Matthew 11:28.

13. Isaiah 12:2.

14. James 1:19.

15. Matthew 7:7.

16. Matthew 6:34.

17. Matthew 6:14.

Chapter 9   Waiting on the Lord

1. Isaiah 2:3.

2. Ibid.